320.973
S338b

350.6

78-599

320.973

P9-BVX-476

THE BETRAYERS

by

Phyllis Schlafly

and

Chester Ward

Rear Admiral, United States Navy (Ret.)

Pere Marquette Press
Alton, Illinois

© Copyright, 1968   by Phyllis Schlafly

All rights reserved. No portion of this book may be reproduced in any form without written permission from the copyright owner, except for the inclusion of brief quotations in a review.

First Printing, October 1968

Printed in the United States of America

TABLE OF CONTENTS

2472

chapter I

NOT SICK – BUT BETRAYED

It became clear beyond further concealment, by the summer of Sixty-eight, that America has been betrayed. Betrayed, indeed, on so many fronts, with such a synchronized time schedule, that it is no longer possible to believe that all our weaknesses in the face of internal and external threats are the result of accident or coincidence. The only open question is whether the interwoven fabric of betrayal was the work of fools or dupes or traitors – or of all three groups combined.

Our cities have become more dangerous than the jungles infested by Viet Cong guerrillas. Serious crime has gone up 88% in eight years. Each year it is worse: 1967 showed a shocking 16% increase over 1966.[1] Our parks are wilder than the frontier towns of 150 years ago and, for women, far more fearful. Our senior citizens have lost their security of person and of savings. Our children are not safe at a school football game or the local movie theater.

On all sides we witness a spineless surrender to violence – to rioters, looters, arsonists, murderers, rapists, street mobs, university students carrying obscene signs, "peace" demonstrators, pornographers, revolutionaries, and blackmailers.

The President's own commission admitted that the domestic crisis in our land is the most alarming since the Civil War.

Our economic system and our savings are on

the skids because of galloping inflation (in mid-1968 the annual rate was 6%), the gold drain, and the highest interest rates in half a century.

In 1960, John F. Kennedy campaigned against the alleged decline in "our image abroad." In 1968, after eight years of the present Administration, our image abroad is the lowest in our history. The capture of the Pueblo by North Korea on January 23, 1968 is the worst humiliation our nation has ever suffered. It was an act of naked piracy such as the United States did not tolerate even when we were a new and tiny country huddled along the Atlantic coast.

The Pueblo was not seized by a great naval power but by a fifth-rate puppet of the Soviet Union. The response of the Johnson-Humphrey Administration for seven months was to crawl to the Communists with abject appeals to them to accept our apologies and even keep the ship and its valuable equipment, if only the crew could be released. Meanwhile, the 82 crewmen languished in a Communist prison, insulted before the world.

On August 28, 1968 the U.S. Ambassador to Guatemala was machine-gunned to death by Cuban-backed Communists. The chauffeur reported the gory details:

"He was lying on the ground and still moving, so they shot him some more times with pistols until he died."[2]

He is the first American ambassador in our history to be assassinated. Not since the days of the Roman Empire, when respect for the person of ambassadors was imposed upon even the most retarded of barbarians, has the ambassador of a great nation been treated so savagely.

This is only the latest humiliating harassment

inflicted upon the United States by the Communist dictator of Cuba, who had five U.S. planes hijacked and flown to Havana at pistol-point. American citizens are no longer safe from Castro when flying in American planes over American soil.

Who is to blame for the state of our nation?

Everywhere, people are beating their breasts and saying "society" is sick — sick with crime, confusion, complacency, and lack of compassion. When a criminal is apprehended, we are told he is *not* to blame — it is the fault of a selfish and insensitive society. When arsonists burn our cities, we are told by the Kerner Report that the real culprit is "white racism" and the wrongs of 100 years ago. When corruption in Government is exposed, we are told we should blame the apathy of the voters.

It is fashionable to excuse national mistakes by saying that "we" are at fault. To avoid charges of partisan politics or "witch-hunting," speakers are supposed to diffuse responsibility by saying that "we" failed at the Bay of Pigs, "we" let the North Koreans capture the Pueblo, and "we" have made mistakes in Vietnam.

Let's call a halt to this passion to pass the buck to "society" or to the American people as a whole. Guilt is *not* collective — guilt is personal.

The cringing appeasement of our Government in dealing with the Communists — whether in Moscow or Paris or Cuba or North Korea or Vietnam — is not the fault of society or circumstances. It is specifically and personally the fault of the officials who have misrepresented us.

The American people are tired of having all their ills and defeats blamed on the poor longsuffering citizens, the parents, and the taxpayers.

The overwhelming majority of Americans are God-fearing, law-abiding, honest, and generous. The record proves that we have been warm-hearted and openhanded to the less fortunate at home and abroad.

We had a right to expect our officials to "insure domestic tranquility" — but they shed crocodile tears for the rights of the criminals, and turned a deaf ear to the cries of their victims.

We gave our sons and husbands and brothers to fight 10,000 miles away in Vietnam — and we had a right to expect that our GIs would be backed to the limit with weapons and policies which would bring victory in the shortest time with the least cost in lives. But our officials have permitted the war to drag on and on and on, in a "no-win" stalemate that betrays the supreme sacrifice our boys are making.

With all the fantastic amount of money we gave the Johnson Administration for military defense, we had a right to expect that no aggressor would be permitted to imperil our security. But this Administration scrapped the great superiority we had eight years ago and has permitted the Soviet nuclear arsenal to surpass us and to threaten the very survival of our nation.

Do you really think that America could have been brought to her present condition by coincidence or by honest mistakes? Don't logic and facts force you to the same conclusion Abraham Lincoln reached in his great "House Divided" speech?

"But when we see a lot of framed timber, different portions of which we know have been gotten out at different times and places and by different workmen . . . and when we see these timbers joined together, and see they exactly make the frame of a house or a mill, all the tenons and mortises exactly fitting, . . . in such a case, we find it impossible not to believe that . . . all understood one another from the beginning, and all *worked upon a common plan.*"[3]

Just as fools could not be the architects of a spacious and beautiful house, so fools could not devise and carry out a complex and ingenious plan for destroying all parts of the great American Republic in different ways at one critical time. Logic and facts force us to the conclusion that America has been betrayed — to criminals at home and to Communists abroad.

It is not hard to identify those who have betrayed us to criminals. They are the cowardly public officials who fail to enforce the law. This includes the Mayors and Governors who handcuff the local police, the prosecuting attorneys who fail to prosecute, the judges who fail to hand down the proper sentences, the Supreme Court Justices who set criminals and Communists free, and Attorney General Ramsey Clark who is bugling retreat from law enforcement.

Nor is it hard to find the remedy. Dealing with criminals takes (1) the physical power necessary to restore law and order, and (2) the will to use it. We have the former; we are wanting the latter. The police, the laws, and the prisons are ready and waiting. All that is required is public officials who honor the citizen rather than the criminal, the lawful rather than the lawless, Americans rather than Communists, decency rather than pornography, God rather than atheism.

New appointments to the Supreme Court will take longer, but the Justices are known to "follow the election returns" and, if a new Administration is elected, a change in decisions could come even before vacancies occur.[4]

The reason for the incredible weakness our country has so often displayed in international affairs is that not only have the betrayers in Washington demonstrated they have no *will* to use our strength (by winning in Vietnam, demanding the return of the Pueblo, enforcing the Monroe Doctrine, etc.) — but the betrayers also have deprived our nation of so much strategic nuclear *power* that it is impossible for the U.S. to deal from strength either on the battlefield or at the bargaining table.

Even if we have good men in our Government, and surely there are many, they cannot save our country because we do not have the nuclear superiority which alone will enable us to deal from strength.

It is obvious that the result has been appeasement and retreat from Communism everywhere in the world. What is not so obvious — but far more dangerous — is what this means for the lives of 200,000,000 Americans.

Our nation could not have been brought so low in eight years by fuzzy-minded, muddle-headed liberals "taken in" by Communist lies and myths. Our present condition was brought about by brilliant and calculating men who "worked upon a common plan." They are extremely cunning and powerful. Hardly anyone wants to point the finger at them because of the tremendous power they wield in the Department of Defense — they have more Federal money to spend than all other Government departments combined. These betrayers must be identified and repudiated because they are endangering our very survival as a free nation.

And this must be done in 1968 on the over-riding principle of "the most serious threat." When we talk about the dangers to the American system from economic collapse or political subversion or infiltration, the crisis may not come to a head within four years, or even more. But when we talk about danger from nuclear attack or blackmail by the Soviets, the crisis is upon us in 1968.

Wouldn't you like to know *how* our officials have betrayed us? Even more important, wouldn't you like to know *why* they are betraying us — and what their betrayal means to your future and the future of your children? Wouldn't you like to know how the Soviet invasion of Czechoslovakia reveals America's betrayers as they have never been revealed before? That is what this book is all about, and we will "tell it like it is."

chapter II

WHY DO THEY BETRAY US?

Attacks against Americans on the home front reached a climax in Chicago at the end of August 1968. Disgraceful disorders dominated the Democratic National Convention, both inside and outside the meeting. The political party which asks to govern our nation for another four years proved incapable of governing itself.

More than 25,000 police, National Guardsmen, State and Federal troops were called in to maintain order. This is approximately one law-enforcement officer per Democrat in attendance at the Convention.

The weapons used against the Chicago police by 3,000 filthy, foul-mouthed Yippies, hippies and chippies included water pistols containing lye water, spray cans of oven cleaner, razor blades affixed in shoe tips, blocks of wood with long spikes imbedded in them, ax handles, balls studded with nails, black widow spiders, and brownpaper bags and balloons filled with human waste which burst when they hit the police. The revolutionaries were organized by professionals, including at least ten known Communists, and their press releases charging "police brutality" were printed three weeks ahead of time.[1]

In spite of the most intense provocation, plus the fact that 118 policemen were hospitalized and scores of others wounded, not a single demonstrator was killed or seriously injured.

Inside the Convention hall, a shocking 1,041 Delegates voted for a so-called Vietnam "peace plank" which would have been exactly the "camouflaged surrender" against which President Eisenhower warned. It required all the political muscle of the Johnson Administration to vote down the "surrender now" Delegates. What the peaceniks could not secure by votes, they sought to seize by coercion and confusion.

While hundreds of Party Delegates and their young friends in the streets of Chicago raised shrill cries for surrender to the 5th-rate Communist half-state of North Vietnam, much more far-reaching betrayals of America were being planned and executed in Washington. Hard at work there were the unelected bureaucrats, the self-styled "intellectuals" and "whiz kids" who had used the Democratic Party to take over control of the White House, the State Department and even the Pentagon. Nearing completion of their first 8-year plan, they were working on a 4-year extension which they hoped the 1968 elections would give.

These betrayers have already scrapped more than half our former strategic military might. Conclusive proof of this, with full authoritative documentation, is presented in Chapters VI and VII. The only question remaining open is, *why* are they doing it?

Many informed Americans have wrestled with this question. They find it impossible to believe that our leaders could be so stupid as to fall for Communist lies and promises. On the other hand, it is equally impossible to believe that America's leaders are all Communists or knowingly aiding the Communists. No doubt, there is substantial Communist and pro-Communist penetration of Washington. But there could not be enough Communists in positions of sufficient influence to plan and implement the national suicidal foreign and defense policies which have plagued us with such consistency for the past 8 years.

Yet, America is being betrayed. It follows, therefore, that there must be betrayers in influential positions in order to bring America down so fast in so short a time. If these men are not fools or Communist traitors, what are they? Why have they not been exposed?

The reason why the betrayers have not been detected and identified is, strangely, because most Americans are strongly anti-Communist. The post-World War II exposure of proof that Soviet agents such as Alger Hiss, Harry Dexter White and the Rosenbergs had stolen our defense and diplomatic secrets, convinced us of the great danger from Communist infiltration.

At this point, a non sequitur was accepted by most knowledgeable Americans. We jumped from the entirely valid proposition that all Communists are betraying our country, to the non sequitur that all those betraying our country must be Communists. Up until 1960, this was coincidentally true — the major internal threat to America, on all fronts, did indeed stem from Communists and pro-Communist traitors.

The New Breed

When the new Kennedy-Johnson Administration took office in January 1961, a new breed of betrayers flooded into the Federal Government. They immediately took control of and reversed the defense policies of the United States.

What these men were doing to America's military strength became apparent to experts shortly after the Cuban missile crisis in October 1962. It was apparent to most knowledgeable Americans by 1964. But *why* they were doing it still remains a mystery to most Americans.

Most Americans are so convinced that no one but a Communist or pro-Communist would betray America to the Soviet Union that they exonerate the motives of every Government official who is obviously *not* a Communist. Most Americans reason that because Robert McNamara, Paul Nitze, and others in control of our defense policies are *not* Communists, they could not betray America.

Thus when these men favored the Communists (as they always did), and reduced the military power of the United States vis-a-vis the Soviet Union (as they always did), our military experts and knowledgeable anti-Communists criticized them only as being "naive," as desiring to stake our hope for peace on Communist promises instead of on U.S. military strength, and as stupidly believing (against all evidence) that the Soviets are "mellowing."

The paradox was that, all the time, we were the ones who were too naive — too trusting and tolerant of the motives of the leaders in our Government.

The new breed of betrayers was only *pretending* to be deceived by the Communists, *pretending* to trust in Soviet treaties, *pretending* to believe that the Kremlin bosses were "mellowing," *pretending* to be idealistic "one-worlders," instead of deliberate betrayers.

America's betrayers are not fools, they are not

naive and trusting, they are not stupid enough to believe the Soviets are "mellowing." The betrayers are not appeasing the Soviets because they "trust" them to keep their agreements, but for exactly the opposite reason. The betrayers know that the Soviets are *not* mellowing and will never depart from their drive for world conquest — and that the Kremlin bosses (who have no regard for human life or their treaties) intend to "bury" us in the most efficient way: by the use of nuclear weapons against the United States — unless we surrender first.

Thus it was that our military experts, our patriotic Congressmen, and informed anti-Communists kept very busy over the years since 1960, proving again and again that our leaders are "blind" or "taken in" or "mistaken." As a result, the betrayers have never been accused of anything more than stupidity or incompetence or naivete. And that is exactly what the betrayers are not!

Take the outstanding case of Robert Strange McNamara. Nearly every one of the retired members of the Joint Chiefs of Staff and senior military commanders who has spoken out, has written books or articles demonstrating conclusively, on the basis of evidence and expertise, that all McNamara's major policies were "wrong," "mistaken," "dangerous," and "based on false and foolish premises." Our military experts have proved that all McNamara's programs led to reducing U.S. strategic military power and even rendering U.S. tactical military power ineffective, as in Vietnam. Congressional committee reports have proved the same. Sometimes, McNamara's critics go so far as to charge him with "deceit," but that is all.

The fact is that McNamara is a brilliant man who had a definite objective, and who never made a major mistake in his efforts to achieve it. All his policy decisions were completely consistent, and each of them contributed to his overall plan — the destruction of U.S. strategic nuclear striking power.

The Treacherous Four-Word Formula

If these men are not naive or misguided idealists, and if they are not Communist or pro-Communist traitors, *why* are they betraying America? Why are so many Americans, on so many fronts, betraying America?

"The pen is mightier than the sword," according to the ancient aphorism which antedates the invention of gunpowder; but in the nuclear-space age, how do words weigh against megatons?

The U.S. nuclear arsenal in 1962 contained some fifty thousand million tons of TNT-explosive-power equivalent. A treacherous four-word formula has been the moving force in liquidating *half* of this arsenal, or more than twenty-five thousand million tons of deliverable explosive power; many more million tons are scheduled to disappear soon. The motivation of the betrayers who planned and supervised this fantastic scrapping of U.S. strength can be summed up in four fatal words: "Rather Red than dead."

The average patriotic American identifies this famous slogan as associated either (1) with the Communist propagandists, or (2) with the bearded beatniks and voluble Vietniks, the kind who carry placards reading "Make love, not war," and don't appear capable of doing either.

Actually, the Satanically-clever masters of psychological warfare in the Kremlin have used this four-word slogan to appeal to the intellectuals, particularly to those knowledgeable enough to comprehend the destructive capabilities of nuclear weapons. The slogan "Rather Red than dead" has harnessed man's desire for self-preservation. This slogan has also harnessed the cumulative power of the excessive cowardice of a few men, the guilt-feelings of many men, and the normal fears of all men. This slogan has harnessed these forces together so effectively that they are dragging our nation into surrender to the Communists.

"Rather Red than dead" is a double swindle. In the present time period, it is the familiar trick of logic known as the "false alternative." We do *not* have to choose between being Red or dead. We can choose a third course, namely, being strong and free.

But, because of the tremendous lead-time it takes to build nuclear weapons, once the Soviets move into a position of clear superiority, then America will have no option at all. We will no longer even be able to choose whether we will be Red or dead because the Soviets will have the power to make that decision for us. They may prefer to have us dead than Red. In any event, it will be the Kremlin's choice to make, not ours, because the power will be in Soviet hands. So, the "Rather Red than dead" slogan swindles Americans now and in the future.

Does this mean that anyone who would rather be Red than dead is a traitor or betrayer? No, it doesn't. But to be a patriot, a man would certainly have to be willing to take reasonable and even very serious *risks* of death in preference to becoming Red. He would have to be willing to take similar risks to prevent the stark Red-or-dead choice from being forced upon him or his fellow Americans, his family, and even our allies. Many brave men are fighting and dying in Vietnam for exactly this reason.

This distinction has been recognized for centuries in the law of war and in the administration of our armed forces. A fighting man is not a coward or a traitor if he surrenders when he no longer has a fighting chance to resist and would surely lose his life if he did. Many brave and honorable men have become prisoners of war under those circumstances.

On the other hand, if a member of the armed services "deserts in the face of the enemy," if he surrenders on his own volition rather than take his chances in a fight, he is indeed liable to court-martial and to punishment up to death, if a state of war is legally recognized.

Many of the captive nations were faced with the actual choice of being Red or dead. They cannot be blamed for submitting to Soviet slavery when they had no rational alternative.

Our Government officials are bound by their oath of office to "support and defend the Constitution of the United States against all enemies, foreign or domestic" and to take that oath "with no mental reservations whatsoever." We pay these officials and entrust them with awesome powers in order that they can fulfill their duties to keep America so strong that we will never be either Red or dead.

Thus, it is no more than fair to call men betrayers if they breach their duty by disarming, instead of defending, the United States. In deciding not to take the *risk* of competing with the Soviet Union for strategic nuclear strength, and in acting on that decision contrary to their sworn duty and responsibility, they have certainly betrayed our country — and the proof is available in what they have done to our nation's defenses.

Actually, Paul Nitze, now Deputy Secretary of Defense, in a speech in 1960, quite frankly pointed out how the Executive could avoid the U.S. Constitutional safeguards of Senate approval of treaties and agreements with foreign nations, by taking "unilateral actions" instead of signing "pieces of paper."

The betrayers have looked the awful destructive power of the hydrogen bomb in the face, and they have made their choice. They *think* they have chosen to be Red rather than risk being dead. Actually, the only choice they have made is to make America weak rather than strong — in the hope that the Soviets will want them Red rather than dead.

To insure their own skins, the betrayers are depriving all Americans of any other choice. If, instead of being betrayed into the power of the Kremlin to make you Red or dead, you would rather rebuild America's strength to keep yourself alive and free, then it is up to you to do something about it before it is too late.

chapter III

WHY THE SOVIETS INVADED CZECHOSLOVAKIA

At 11 P.M. on the night of Tuesday, August 20, 1968, the Soviet Union suddenly invaded Czechoslovakia with massive troops and tanks. The importance of this event *to every American* ranks with the Cuban Missile Crisis of 1962.

The liberals were temporarily caught off base by this crude act of the Soviets. It proved again the utter foolishness of the entire liberal line about Communism.

Even a Soviet diplomat at the United Nations moaned in dismay, "Did we really *have* to do this?"

The answer is simple. No, the Soviets did not *have* to do this at all. The Soviets were not in the slightest d a n g e r — ideologically, politically, or militarily — from Czechoslovakia. Czech Communist Party boss Dubcek had already substantially capitulated to Soviet policies and demands. His first official act upon assuming his post had been to fly to Moscow to get his orders from the Kremlin. He had declared that the alliance with the Soviets was the "Alpha and Omega" of Czech policy, he was moving to curb the press, and had already ousted officials to whom the Kremlin objected. When notified of the invasion, Dubcek cried in anguish:

"How could they do this to me? I have served the cause of the Soviet Union and Communism all my life."[1]

There was not the slightest need for an armed invasion. Some 800 Soviet officers were already on duty as "advisers" to the Czech army. They commanded all strategic and logistic planning, conducted the maneuvers, and determined the Czech officers' pay and promotion. The Soviets controlled all supplies of gasoline and diesel fuel oil used by Czech industries. About 60,000 troops were always kept poised on the adjacent Hungarian frontier, 300,000 in East Germany, and panzer divisions in Poland.

The theory of some commentators that the Soviets were worried about liberal "ideas" in Czechoslovakia simply does not accord with reality. "Ideas" are of minimal importance in the face of such overwhelming military forces as the Soviets had over the Czechs.

Nor did the Soviets have to use such a tremendous invasion army. The Czech Defense Minister, General Martin Dzur, told a secret session of his government that the Soviets used 650,000 occupation troops.[2] In addition, the Soviets used thousands of tanks, armored cars, trucks, self-propelled artillery and rocket-launchers—against a people with practically no weapons and an army of only 175,000. The Soviets moved more troops into Czechoslovakia *in five days* than the Johnson Administration has moved into Vietnam *in five years* — and the Soviets did it with complete surprise.

What The Invasion Revealed

The invasion of Czechoslovakia demonstrated how much the cunning war-planners in the Kremlin have learned since their invasion of Hungary 12 years ago. In 1956, the Soviets sent in military forces which were *superior* to resistance from the Hungarian Freedom Fighters. The Soviets won, of course, but their victory cost much bloodshed and destruction. Many potential industrial-worker-slaves were killed, and waves of criticism of the Soviet Union swept around the world.

The Kremlin learned its lesson well. Against Czechoslovakia, the Soviets used military force which was not merely superior, but *overwhelmingly* superior.

Whereas the Hungarians were able to put up a valiant struggle against the Soviet invaders and win some temporary victories, the Czechs had "no rational alternative" to immediate surrender. The Hungarians believed they had a fighting chance to escape enslavement — and they took it, thereby creating a two-sided "war," or "exchange" of military attacks. The Czechs, on the other hand, faced by *overwhelming* instead of merely superior military force, saw that they did not have even a fighting chance of escaping destruction if they resisted, and so they surrendered without using any military power whatsoever against the aggressors. Thus, there was no "exchange." A "war" was averted, and there was substantially no bloodshed. The Russian press boasted that the Czechs "love the Soviet army."[3]

All this, of course, involved "conventional" military weapons — that is, non-nuclear power. With strategic nuclear weapons, the principle is the same, and the potential results are the same, but *magnified 10,000,000 times*.

We are fortunate that the invasion of Czechoslovakia has given us a perfect lesson which explains the motivation of Paul Nitze, Robert Mc-Namara, Walt Rostow, Roswell Gilpatric, and the other gravediggers.* By 1961, when they all first flooded into U.S. Government offices, this was the way they reasoned:

1) The prime objective is to avoid nuclear war, a "nuclear exchange," because that would mean death and destruction.

2) Unless one side could be so reduced in nuclear power that it obviously does not have a "fighting chance" against the other, the gravediggers felt that a "nuclear exchange" was inevitable.

3) The United States could not indefinitely retain overwhelming nuclear superiority over the U.S.S.R. because of the Kremlin's ambition for world domination. By 1961, the Soviets had already beaten the U.S. in producing the first ICBM and the first man-made satellite. Our intelligence reported that the Soviets were exploiting their greater rocket thrust and space payload capabilities for use in nuclear weapons.

4) The gravediggers realized they had no way of reducing the Soviet nuclear arsenal. They knew perfectly well that Soviet treaties are worthless. The gravediggers know that, when the Soviets feel strong enough, they will either launch an attack against us or demand our surrender because they are bent on world conquest.

5) The gravediggers feared that if, at that time, the U.S. had sufficient nuclear striking power,

---

*"Gravediggers" is a precise term used in this and other books by the authors to describe the men who advocate U.S. nuclear disarmament. In doing this, they are really digging our graves which will enable the men in the Kremlin to push us in.

we might take our "fighting chance" and launch whatever nuclear weapons we had rather than surrender. Paul Nitze explained it at the Asilomar National Strategy Seminar on April 29, 1960 with an analogy to poker:

> "In a poker game with several players, what is the most dangerous hand? Not the worst hand, but the second best hand. With the second best hand, one is tempted to follow up the betting, but if one does, one gets clobbered."

The gravediggers did not want to run the risk of getting "clobbered" with nuclear weapons. They would rather be Red than even risk being dead.

6) Therefore, from that day onward, Nitze, McNamara and the other gravediggers devoted their plans and their actions to insure that the U.S. would be reduced from the "best" hand, to the "second best hand," to a hand which is so weak that we would never be "tempted to follow up the betting" in the nuclear game with the Soviet Union.

Thus, the Nitze plan enunciated in 1960, and carried out in detail by Nitze and McNamara from 1961 through 1968, was designed for the sole purpose of making sure that the United States would have "no rational alternative" to surrender to the Soviet *overwhelming* nuclear striking force — just as the Czechs had "no rational alternative" to surrender to the Soviet overwhelming conventional forces.

The principle of overwhelming military force worked on the Czechs with conventional weapons — and it will work just as well with nuclear weapons. The Nitze-McNamara policies will leave us as naked of defense against Soviet nuclear mis-

siles as the Czechs were against Soviet tanks —
only able to shake our fists at the missiles as they
plunge toward us from outer space.

The Rehearsal

Since the Soviets did not *have* to invade Czechoslovakia, why did they do it? The explanation
is not ideological, as we have seen, but military:
not *defensive* military, but in preparation for a
major *offensive*. The Soviets did it because it
served four important purposes.

First, the Soviet invasion of Czechoslovakia was
a rehearsal for military action. It gave the Soviet
and Warsaw Pact armies actual practice for an
invasion by surprise. It not only foreshadows the
Soviet takeover of all Europe — it was a military
exercise in how it is to be done with speed, precision, and no damage to the Soviet forces *or* to
the industries and cities which are the "spoils"
of occupation.

Correspondents in Prague expressed amaze-
ment at the efficiency of the Soviet airborne and
ground operations, saying that Hitler unopposed
never moved his panzer divisions so fast. Columns
of tanks were moved swiftly over confusing sec-
ondary roads without traffic jams. The Soviets
even landed a communications plane and a plane
of personnel in civilian clothes hours ahead of the
invasion, who were welcomed by Russian embassy staff in Prague.

It should be noted that there was no accident
or provocation or miscalculation which caused
the invasion. It was done "in cold blood" with
the disciplined coordination of four satellite
armies. Nor did the Soviets worry about offending
world opinion. They made their plans to reach
their objective, and then coldly carried them out.

According to the Czech Defense Minister, the invasion required six months of planning and logistical preparation.

The Probe

Secondly, the Soviet invasion of Czechoslovakia was a probe to establish and verify these important points of military information: that NATO is bankrupt of military power and completely helpless; that the United Nations can only "play games," and will not do even that if it might annoy the U.S.S.R.; and that the U.S. strategic deterrent has completely lost its credibility in Europe. The invasion demonstrated that the present paralysis of NATO, of the UN, and of the U.S. in Europe, would have been the same if the Soviets had, in a similar sudden way, taken Austria, West Berlin, West Germany, or all or part of Western Europe. The press was full of comments about the "passive" attitude of the United States. *Time* magazine said:

"Washington's reaction had about it an almost dreamlike unreality in its restraint. . . . The relative lack of polemics was remarkable."

The reason for the loss of the credibility of our strategic deterrent is that Nitze and McNamara have scrapped our nuclear superiority (described in detail in Chapter VI).

On August 31, the U.S. State Department issued a statement which declared that the Soviets had upset the military balance in Europe by their invasion of Czechoslovakia, and concluded: "The status quo has been changed."[4] It was not the invasion which changed the "status quo" — it was what Nitze and McNamara did to our nuclear deterrent that changed it. The invasion only revealed it for everyone to see.

The Soviet invasion of Czechoslovakia established for the world to see exactly *who has whom* deterred. The men in the Kremlin did not worry at all about "starting World War III" — the way Lyndon Johnson worried about starting it when he permitted the bombing of minor targets in North Vietnam.

The Soviet invasion also established another vital piece of military information — that U.S. intelligence, including all the intelligence supposedly picked up by our satellite surveillance, is entirely inadequate. U.S. diplomatic and defense personnel were taken by surprise — despite the fact that the invasion required the coordinated mass movements of 250,000 troops from five countries as the surprise "spearhead," plus another 400,000 troops as reinforcements.

We are always told that we have embassies, legations and consulates in Communist countries in order to secure valuable intelligence. Yet, the Communists take our State and Defense Departments by surprise in every international crisis.

The Signal

Third, the Soviet invasion of Czechoslovakia was a "signal" to the U.S. gravediggers — the men who are feverishly working for drastic U.S. nuclear disarmament. By the invasion, the Soviets provided a dramatic object lesson in the Kremlin's bold determination to use force not only when necessary, but when convenient.

This "signal" swept away any possible doubts in the minds of the gravediggers that preemptive surrender is the only safe way to avert a Soviet attack with overwhelming force. "Overwhelming force" against the United States would have to be strategic nuclear force, which in turn means a surprise massive nuclear attack destroying the majority of our population and weapons.

At the same time, the Soviet invasion of Czechoslovakia was another "signal" to the gravediggers which reinforced them in their belief that they would rather be Red than risk being dead. The invasion was an object lesson to convince the gravediggers that surrender to the Soviets' overwhelming military force is not so bad after all. The Soviets showed their "restraint" and "compassion" by not mass-murdering tens of thousands of Czechs, and by returning some of the Dubcek administration officials to government positions.

Using the combination of the carrot and the club, the Kremlin is thus telling the gravediggers that, if they do succeed in bringing the United States to the point of surrender without nuclear resistance, the gravediggers may be allowed to retain their present Government positions. This offer would be tempting to some of the power-hungry egomaniacs in our Government who believe that the American people are "too damned dumb to understand,"[5] and that the U.S. Constitution is "outmoded" and unduly restrains the Executive.[6] The top ones might even have *more* power as heads of a Soviet satellite, and they wouldn't be bothered with the "old-fashioned" American electoral process. As demonstrated in Czechoslovakia, the Kremlin not only puts those subservient to the Soviet Union in positions of power — it keeps them there.

The Soviet invasion of Czechoslovakia proved again that no one with any common sense could possibly believe the gravediggers' line about the Soviets' "mellowing," desiring only "peaceful coexistence," and "converging" with the U.S. in some kind of one-world togetherness. The Soviet invasion proved that Communism *is* "monolithic" and that it is *not* run by reasonable men in "gray-flannel suits." The Soviet invasion proved that, if we are so foolish as to "build bridges" to Communism (as President Johnson urged in his State of the Union message), the Reds will simply use those bridges to march their troops over. The Soviet invasion proved the utter worthlessness of treaties with the Soviets because they broke their 1968 agreement with the Czechs within weeks of making it.[7]

Yet the gravediggers continue to mouth these fatuous falsehoods. Senator Joseph Clark said we need no anti-missile defense because we can rely upon the "compassion" of the Soviets. The Soviet doublecross of Czechoslovakia in no way cooled the lust of the gravediggers for new nuclear disarmament agreements with the Kremlin. President Johnson continued to petition the Kremlin bosses for a summit conference and for "progress" with negotiations to "freeze" production of offensive and defensive missile systems.[8] That oracle of the Liberal Establishment, *The New York Times* columnist James Reston, pleaded:

"We do have to talk to the Russians about arms control even though we despise their savage and clumsy invasion of Czechoslovakia. The Johnson Administration has no difficulty with this argument. . . . The line of communication therefore has to be reopened with Moscow on the great questions of war and peace, no matter how stupid and cruel they have been in Czechoslovakia."[9]

The Test

Finally, the Soviet invasion of Czechoslovakia enabled the Kremlin to take an up-to-the-minute test of U.S. will to resist. The Soviets never leave anything to chance; they plan and test, replan and retest.

Before Khrushchev made his decision to send nuclear missiles into Cuba in 1962, he carefully tested President Kennedy's will to resist. He met him in Vienna in 1961 and took his measure there. Later, he sent a message to Kennedy via the poet, Robert Frost, which said: "You are too liberal to fight, even in defense of your vital interests."[10] Receiving no response, Khrushchev correctly guessed that there would be no real retaliation against his sending nuclear missiles into Cuba, so he had everything to gain and nothing to lose by making the big move.

The big test, however, was the building of the Berlin Wall in August 1961. The Soviets were fully prepared to back down from completion and fortification of the Wall if the U.S. made the slightest move. But the Soviets struck with surprise and speed and took the West off guard. They started building the Wall on a summer weekend when President Kennedy was vacationing in Hyannis Port. By the time he returned to Washington on Monday afternoon and consulted with the State Department, the Berlin Wall was a fait accompli.

Now, by moving such huge forces into Czechoslovakia, the Soviets are in position to invade all of West Germany with great speed and short supply lines. Indeed the Czechs have warned us that the Soviets may seize West Berlin at any time.[11]

The Soviets started their 1968 tests by having their North Korean stooges seize the Pueblo and hold its crew. This act of piracy not only served to humiliate the United States before the world, but it proved again that the U.S. is "too liberal to fight, even in defense of its own vital interests" — or even for the lives of our servicemen.

The Soviet invasion of Czechoslovakia in August 1968 could be the final test before the big action to take over all of western Europe. Will the Soviets conclude that our Government is so shot through with "Rather-Red-than-deadism" that the time is ripe to give us and NATO the final surprise?

And — later — what will we do if they launch a surprise attack on the United States itself? What did the Czech people do? They shook their fists at the Soviet tanks. We will be able to do that — and nothing more — when the Soviet hydrogen warheads start their invasion, so far as defense against their missiles is concerned. On July 30, 1968 in San Francisco, Vice President Hubert Humphrey admitted that the United States has "not a single weapon system that can protect us from annihilation."[12] This is the pitiful position of weakness to which McNamara, Nitze, and the Johnson Administration have brought the United States in the last eight years.

Only two weeks after the invasion of Czechoslovakia, Brezhnev began displaying the new strength of his hand. Banner headlines around the world screamed: "Kremlin Warns West Germany: Demands Bonn End 'Hostility.' "[13] By "hostility," the Kremlin means, of course, any opposition to Soviet takeover of all Europe. The crude demands which Soviet Ambassador Semyon Tsarapkin served on West German Chancellor Kurt Kiesinger were so harsh that the Chancellor emerged from the meeting "utterly dejected."

The terms were so inclusive that they amounted to a demand for a camouflaged surrender, without very much camouflage.

People throughout the world are beginning to wake up to the fact that the Soviet move is the beginning of the end of freedom in Europe. Even Brian Beedham, foreign editor of the *London Economist,* long a salesman for "detente" with the Soviets, now asserts that the invasion of Czechoslovakia made most people in Western Europe realize that —

> "in the last resort, nobody except the Americans has the physical power to protect the rest of us against a Russia that behaves like this."[14]

Do we have the physical power to protect ourselves against a Russia that behaves like this? That is the question.

chapter IV

PLANNED DEFEAT

The first clear evidence most Americans had that a new breed of betrayers had moved into control of the defense of our country was the Bay of Pigs defeat in April 1961. A brave band of Cuban Freedom Fighters — encouraged, financed and armed by the U.S., and promised the sea and air support which was essential to the success of the invasion — landed at the Bay of Pigs on the coast of Cuba.

Castro's forces apparently had advance warning of the attack and quickly closed in on the Freedom Fighters. There was no air or sea support to make the invasion succeed or to save the men. Nearly all the Freedom Fighters were killed or captured.

The Bay of Pigs was not only a tragic betrayal of the bravest Cubans, but a military defeat of the first magnitude for the United States.

The American people were shocked and dismayed — but most were sympathetic toward the young President who had been in office only three months. There was a uniform belief that the blood of the Cuban Freedom Fighters would be redeemed by another invasion soon. President Kennedy announced that "we do not intend to abandon" Cuba to the Communists.[1] No one believed that the U.S. would accept this defeat on the battlefield or at the bar of world opinion.

Americans told themselves that a new invasion was only a matter of timing.

Seven and a half years have gone by since the Bay of Pigs, and the blood of the brave Cubans who died there has never been redeemed, nor has there been the slightest attempt to redeem it.

It strains our intelligence to expect us to believe that the defeat at the Bay of Pigs was the result of stupidity or honest mistakes. It was planned to fail by betrayers inside our Government. How this happened is the story of an American patriot named Whiting Willauer.[2]

Whiting Willauer was a brilliant man, a lawyer and a linguist, who had served as U.S. Ambassador to several countries. He had held an important position with General Chennault's Flying Tigers during World War II. Willauer was legal coordinator of Admiral Byrd's second Antarctic expedition. He had held various Government positions including special representative of the President to the Philippines to reconstitute the civilian economy after World War II. He held a pilot's license for multi-engine aircraft, and was an expert diver, having received commendation for rescue work performed at the risk of his own life while he was Ambassador to Honduras. He began his study of Communism and how to fight it in 1938 through a connection with the Dies Committee.

In 1954, on the basis of his practical experience in fighting international Communism, Willauer was appointed Ambassador to Honduras for the specific purpose of helping to bring about the overthrow of the Communist regime in neighboring Guatemala. Willauer was the American in charge of a team consisting of John Puerifoy,

Ambassador Robert Hill, and several CIA men, which accomplished this objective. Allen Dulles gave Willauer a commendation which stated that the Guatemalan revolution could not have succeeded without him.

Willauer was never deceived by Castro. When our State Department and other prominent Americans were lauding Castro as a sincere idealist and as the Abraham Lincoln of Cuba, Willauer accurately judged Castro to be a Communist on the basis of his Communist associates and his use of the same tactics the Chinese Reds used ten years before. Willauer sent a series of reports to the State Department sounding an alarm about Castro, supplemented by a number of trips to Washington at his own expense to advise senior State Department officials.

On December 10, 1960 Willauer was called into Secretary of State Herter's office and told that President Eisenhower had "a very special job" for him. Herter told Willauer:

"There has been going on since March 17, 1960, the preparations of an invasion, backed by the CIA, but run by Cubans. There is quite a lot of doubt about whether this plan is correct, what the timing should be, various problems about pulling the thing together. I want you to be the senior partner of a partnership of two people. Your junior partner will be a top CIA man. And you will report to . . . 'a board of directors' of Under Secretary level. . . . You are to have access to every piece of information, you are not to do anything in writing that you can avoid putting down on paper. But get in there and take a good hard look at this thing. Give us your real opinion on it."

The Eisenhower Administration realized that a

terrible mistake had been made in allowing Castro to come to power — and made complete plans to rectify that mistake by helping the Cubans to get rid of Castro.

On December 15, 1960 Willauer started work on the Bay of Pigs invasion as the *top* representative of the U.S. Government. He made suggestions about air cover for the invasion. He saw to it that the Joint Chiefs of Staff were advised about invasion plans. He consulted with the American pilots who trained the Cuban pilots for the invasion. He operated on the premise that "this thing should not be done or undertaken unless there was practically no chance it would fail, and that we should have to commit ourselves in advance to see that it was backed up, so that it could not fail."

Everything was running smoothly until January 1961 when the Eisenhower-Nixon Administration was replaced by the Kennedy-Johnson team. On Sunday, January 22, 1961, Whiting Willauer attended "a full dress meeting, chaired by Secretary of State Rusk, attended by the Secretary of Defense [McNamara], and many other high officials, including Allen Dulles and the Chief of the Joint Chiefs of Staff, General Lemnitzer." The whole Bay of Pigs invasion plan was reviewed.

Four days later, Secretary Dean Rusk personally telephoned Willauer and asked him if he would continue in the same capacity in which he had been serving. Willauer said he would be glad to, as he felt very strongly about the need to eliminate the Communist base 90 miles off our coast.

On February 8 at 11:30 A.M. Willauer was called to a meeting in Secretary of State Rusk's office, attended by A. A. Berle, Thomas Mann,

Chester Bowles and Theodore Achilles. This meeting was called preparatory to a conference President Kennedy was to have that afternoon at 3 o'clock to review the invasion plans. Willauer discussed the invasion plans, but it became apparent to him that the others were not primarily interested in this. Willauer's main interest was to make the invasion a success, while the others were much more concerned with what other countries would *think* of the invasion. When the meeting broke up, the men walked to Berle's office. Berle went in first, followed by Achilles and Mann. Berle then turned to Willauer and said: "You are not needed."

About February 15 Willauer felt that the plans for the Bay of Pigs invasion had progressed to where he needed to talk to the CIA in order to complete arrangements for the jet cover for the invasion. He arranged an appointment for a few days later with the appropriate officials in the CIA. On the day before the appointment, Tracy Barnes of the CIA, who was serving as Willauer's junior partner in the Bay of Pigs invasion plans, telephoned Willauer and said: "We can't talk to you any more. We can only talk to other people." This was the only official word Willauer had that he was cut out of the Bay of Pigs invasion plans.

Secretary Rusk was out of the country at the SEATO Conference, so Willauer tried to see Under Secretary Chester Bowles. Willauer called Bowles' secretary every day for 30 days straight, but was unable to secure an appointment. One day Willauer met Bowles in the hall. Bowles said, "I am awfully busy, I will see you later." But he never did. Willauer met Berle a couple of times and asked Berle what he was supposed to do.

Berle said, "I don't know." Willauer finally realized that he was being given the general runaround and had been frozen out of all preparation for the Bay of Pígs invasion.

Willauer recognized that a new Administration was entitled to make its own appointments. But it amazed him that, as a senior career officer, he was fired from his job without being permitted to give anyone the benefit of his vast years of experience and his careful study of the Bay of Pigs invasion plans and preparations.

Because Willauer was not kept in charge, the Swan Island radio station "somehow" failed to broadcast the signal alerting the Cuban underground to revolt; the Lignum Vitae Island radio station was forbidden to tell the Escambray guerrillas to cut the only rail line from Havana to the Bay of Pigs; Castro's air force was not knocked out; some invaders armed with 30-caliber machine guns received 50-caliber ammunition; others armed with Garand rifles received cartridges made for Springfields; paratroopers had no sleep for two nights and no food or water for seven hours before jumping into Cuba; and American warships steamed away without even offering the out-gunned invaders a Dunkirk-type evacuation.

Some months after the Bay of Pigs invasion in April 1961 resulted in total failure, Willauer died of a broken heart, knowing that, had he been kept on the job, people now dead would be alive, and 7 million people would have been liberated from Communism. Willauer had been determined that the Bay of Pigs invasion must succeed — and the evidence points to the conclusion that he was fired from his job by men in our Government who wanted the invasion to fail.

Who were the men in our Government responsible for the decision to let the Bay of Pigs invasion fail? We cannot identify all of them, but we certainly know one of the principals. Five years later, in a frank interview with Stewart Alsop, Secretary of Defense Robert McNamara said about the Bay of Pigs:

"You know damn well where I was at the time of decision — I recommended it."[3]

This planned defeat was not only a disaster for Cuba, but it had two dire results which affected the national security of the United States and the lives of our citizens.

1. The Bay of Pigs failure set the stage for the Cuban missile crisis a year and a half later because it gave the Soviets a nuclear missile base at a "no-warning" distance from the United States. Obviously, if Castro had been overthrown, the Soviets would not have had a missile base in the Western Hemisphere from which they could threaten the lives of Americans with nuclear incineration.

2. The Bay of Pigs failure set the precedent for the betrayers inside our Government to block every plan which would have enforced the Monroe Doctrine and prevented the Soviets from moving their missiles and submarines into Cuba.

Did these men in the State and Defense Departments have a secret reason to want the Soviets to have nuclear missiles and nuclear-armed submarines in Cuba?

chapter V

VICTORY BETRAYED

Most Americans recall with pride the great victory the United States won over the Soviet Communists in the Cuban Missile Crisis of October 1962. Few know, however, that this victory was betrayed — almost immediately; and fewer still know how and by whom it was betrayed. Of those who do, only a handful have had the courage to speak out — to tell the real result and to fix the responsibility. Still outstanding among the few authoritative appraisals is the statement made in 1964 by Richard Nixon:

1. "The operation turned out to be a net gain for the Kremlin."

2. The same group of advisers who had "stayed Kennedy's hand at the Bay of Pigs" again gave "incredibly bad advice . . . which enabled the United States to pull defeat from the jaws of victory."[1]

In the six years since the Cuban Missile Crisis, enough evidence has finally "leaked" to reveal the true story of the interaction between the moves of the Kremlin plotters, and the responses of the "incredibly bad" advisers of President Kennedy.

Can advice be "bad" enough — *unintentionally* — to turn such a massive victory into defeat? If the same group of advisers repeatedly gives "incredibly bad advice" which *always* results in gains for the Communists and losses for the United

States — does not the consistent pattern of the advisers appear far more likely to have been deliberately planned than to have "just happened?"

And then there is the other question asked by so many millions of Americans and to which we never before received a satisfactory answer. How could so many Senators, newspaper writers, Cuban refugees, and even millions of ordinary Americans, know *so many weeks and months before the President of the United States* that the Soviets were sneaking nuclear missiles into Cuba? There was plenty of evidence available from unclassified sources for just plain people to form their own conclusions — and they did so accurately. Senator Kenneth Keating sounded warning after warning in a series of speeches between August 31 and October 12, 1962. Cuban refugees published advertisements in U.S. newspapers reporting the construction of missile pads in Cuba; Miami newspapers detailed the missile buildup for weeks.

Did Administration officials have the opportunity to know more about the missile buildup than the American public? Vastly. By one of the ironies of history, pundit Walter Lippmann, longtime apostle of "accommodation" with the Communists, wrote in his column on October 13, 1962 (just one day before the U-2s took the photographs of the missiles) a pontifical pronouncement that the Administration's intelligence sources were simply so much greater that the State and Defense Departments must be right, and the Senators and the public must be wrong. He stressed:

"Cuba is an island easily within reach of the Navy and Air Force, and with modern apparatus of electronic and photographic intelligence, little of military interest can happen without our knowing it.

"We do not have to guess about what is being landed at Cuban ports or about what is being constructed on Cuban territory. *We know.* And anyone who chooses to question the basis of our present policy must begin by proving that the intelligence estimates are wrong."[2] (emphasis added)

All the objective evidence which has leaked since then clearly proves that although Lippmann was embarrassingly *wrong* about Soviet missiles not being in Cuba, he was *right* that high Administration officials had so much information that they did "not have to guess about what is being landed at Cuban ports." *They knew.*

Many have tried to support the contention that Administration advisers really did not know, or merely in good faith did not believe their own intelligence reports. Some say, "Oh, you know how *U.S.* intelligence is always the last to know!" But *now* we know that the State Department and Pentagon were receiving 50 to 100 reports a day *in the summer of 1962* from the Chief of French Intelligence in the United States, Philippe Thyraud de Vosjoli. According to his reports:

"Most of the evidence pointed in the same direction: that the Russians were indeed bringing in offensive missiles."[3]

The then Under Secretary of State George Ball admitted to a Congressional committee on October 3, 1962 that they knew as far back as July that "military shipments to Cuba suddenly vaulted upward, 85 shiploads arrived in Cuban ports . . . 15 surface-to-air missile sites have been established in the island — the total may eventually reach 25."[4]

We also know now (through a leak in *Newsweek*) that some of our "modern apparatus of electronic intelligence" *before the U-2 photographs were taken* gave positive evidence that Soviet nuclear missile control equipment was in Cuba. U.S. aircraft recorded electronic "signatures" never before picked up outside the area of the Soviet Union itself.

Because of President Kennedy's prompt and patriotic reaction immediately after the first significant U-2 photographs of Soviet missiles were shown to him on October 16, it seems obvious that much earlier intelligence and its interpretation must have been withheld from him. Few would believe that the President himself would have done *nothing* if he had been informed of the enormous evidence of the danger to the American people from offensive nuclear missiles capable of hitting targets almost everywhere in the United States.

That leaves the question, would *any* high Administration official, entrusted with the defense of the lives of all Americans, and having knowledge of Soviet missiles in Cuba targeted at point-blank range against our cities, have merely *done nothing?*

We know the answer to that question. Yes. Robert Strange McNamara, even after examining the U-2 photographs and other intelligence which conclusively proved the presence of the Soviet nuclear missiles, specifically advised the President to *do nothing* about it. According to Roger Hilsman, Director of the State Department Bureau of Intelligence and Research, McNamara argued:

"A missile is a missile. It makes no great difference whether you are killed by a missile fired from the Soviet Union or from Cuba."

Hilsman concluded: "The clear implication of McNamara's position was that the United States should do nothing, but simply accept the presence of Soviet missiles in Cuba and sit tight." According to McNamara, missiles in Cuba "merely permitted the Soviets to begin to close the gap in 1962 rather than a few years later."[5]

Even Paul Nitze challenged this view, saying that missiles in Cuba would cut our warning time from 15 to one or two minutes, so that a sizable part of the U.S. strategic bomber force might be destroyed in a surprise attack. But McNamara stubbornly held to his view.

President Kennedy himself overruled McNamara. Any course of action would involve danger, he conceded, but "the greatest danger of all would be to do nothing."[6] Unfortunately, McNamara then successfully led the group of advisers who persuaded the President to do next-to-nothing, which was only to declare a quarantine, or embargo, against further shipments of Soviet offensive arms to Cuba.

After President Kennedy ordered our Strategic Air Command on alert, we had aircraft and missiles capable of delivering some 50,000,000,000 tons of explosive power on Soviet targets. This was the great shield which protected the lives of Americans from attack by the nuclear missiles the Soviets had sneaked into Cuba. With this vast military power, with the "right" and even so-called "world opinion" on our side, it was a betrayal of the American people and of our national security to make any concessions to the Soviet Union.

But the same advisers who had planned the

defeat at the Bay of Pigs could not tolerate a
victory at the Cuban Missile Crisis. They made a
deal with Khrushchev which sold the 7 million
Cubans into Communist control for the foreseeable future. They betrayed U.S. national security
by *guaranteeing* the U.S.S.R. a strategic base
within the U.S. defense perimeter, in no-warning
range of our cities. They extracted *no* agreement
to protect us against the establishment of Soviet
naval and air bases 90 miles off our coast. They
thus brought Soviet missile and submarine bases
a 10,000-mile trip nearer our most vulnerable
areas.

Senator Barry Goldwater in December 1962
said he was not convinced that the Soviet Union
had removed all its missiles from Cuba, "and I
know of some darned good military men who don't
think so either." He pointed out the probable
use of thousands of Cuban caves.[7] Since then,
Castro has made numerous claims of secret agreements made by the Kennedy Administration. The
Administration has never yet released all the let-
ters and diplomatic correspondence.

Here is the result of the Cuban Missile Crisis
and "confrontation" as summarized in the most
recent comprehensive analysis:

"The United States had the right and the power
to insist on the restoration of the status quo ante
Castro; yet it ended up by paying exorbitantly
for the removal of the sneaked-in weapons. 'The
burglars,' to use President Kennedy's own phrase,
were handsomely rewarded for their crime.

"The American position vis-a-vis world Communism is far weaker than it was before Khrushchev
undertook his Cuban nuclear gamble. However
the results of the 'eyeball-to-eyeball' confronta-

tion may be explained and disguised, they constitute a substantial defeat for the forces of freedom."[8]

We now know that the secret agreements made by the Kennedy Administration at the time of the Cuban Missile Crisis (1) guaranteed Castro against overthrow by any new invasion force, (2) guaranteed the Soviets a missile and submarine base 90 miles off our coast, and (3) did not guarantee the United States anything, even inspection of the missile sites. But were there additional secret surrender terms which have not yet been made public?

You owe it to yourself to study the authoritative evidence presented in Chapters VI and VII. Note the superiority of U.S. nuclear striking power at the time of the Cuban Missile Crisis. Then note exactly when U.S. power started its sharp and consistent plunge downward — and when Soviet power started its equally sharp and steady climb upward. The date is the date of the negotiated settlement which the Kennedy Administration made with the Kremlin. Since that time, U.S. power has been cut by more than half, and is on its way to 1/10th of what it was at the time of the Cuban Missile Crisis.

Was this cut in U.S. nuclear power the fulfillment of a secret surrender pact between the betrayers and the Kremlin in 1962, which was kept secret from the President and the public? Or, was it the result of "unilateral action" by the same advisers "who stayed Kennedy's hand at the Bay of Pigs," and who have been giving "incredibly bad advice" ever since?

chapter VI

THE NITZE SURRENDER PLAN

Revolutionaries, conspirators, traitors, and spies usually conceal their activities by one of two basic techniques.

The first technique is brazenly to tell the totality of their subversive designs — confident that nobody will believe them. Hitler revealed his plans in *Mein Kampf*, and no one listened. Marx and Lenin told the world their goal was world conquest and that "Communists disdain to conceal their views and aims."[1] Few took the Red threat seriously. Khrushchev boasted "we will bury you,"[2] but liberals go through extensive intellectual gyrations to convince themselves that he didn't really mean what he said, even after he put nuclear missiles in Cuba capable of destroying most of the United States.

Rap Brown shouted: "This town should be burned down,"[3] but no one believed him until cities were in flames. The Soviet spies, Guy Burgess and Donald Maclean, both got drunk and at times boasted of their espionage. Maclean would make such remarks as, "I am the English Hiss," and "What would you do if I told you I was working for Uncle Joe?"[4] Until they fled to Moscow, no one took them seriously because it was thought that no Communist would so reveal himself.

The *second* technique of the revolutionaries is

to weave a web of clever lies as a "cover" for their subversive work. This is the way the master spies such as Alger Hiss, Dr. Klaus Fuchs, and Colonel Wennerstroem camouflaged their theft of secret information to transmit to the Soviets.

Paul H. Nitze and Robert S. McNamara — the two men who have controlled U.S. defense during the last eight years — illustrate these two opposite approaches to the identical objective. Nitze stated plainly that his plan would scrap U.S. nuclear superiority and retain only purely retaliatory weapons. McNamara covered with a web of deception the facts (1) that he carried out the Nitze plan for scrapping U.S. nuclear superiority, (2) that McNamara prevented the U.S. from having any actual defense against a Soviet missile attack, and (3) that his entire policy is based on deterring the Soviets by threatening to hit back at them *after* they have killed 150,000,000 Americans.

Working in tandem for the past eight years, Nitze and McNamara have achieved their goal, namely, a revolutionary reversal of the entire defense posture and policy of the United States. Just as they followed a "no-win" policy in the conventional war against the Communists in Vietnam, they adopted a "no-win" policy against the Soviet Union, too, which means they have abandoned even an attempt to maintain a war-winning *capability* in nuclear power.

By restricting U.S. capability to what we can do *after* the Soviets have attacked us with nuclear weapons, the McNamara-Nitze policies have totally reversed the former Joint Chiefs of Staff policy, which was based on the proposition that "forces which cannot win, will not deter."

Nitze, a New York investment banker and member of the Liberal Establishment, laid out the totality of his plan at the famous Asilomar National Strategy Seminar in California in 1960. Speaking on April 29 before an audience of more than 500 scholars and experts on strategy, Nitze made these sensational proposals:

1) that we abandon trying to achieve "a true Class A nuclear capability," and

2) that "we scrap the fixed base vulnerable systems that have their principal utility as components of a Class A capability."[5]

In other words, Nitze proposed that the United States scrap our Class A nuclear weapons and refuse to build new ones of Class A importance.

Nitze went on to propose that this scrapping be accomplished by "a series of unilateral actions." "It would be *hoped*," he said, that the Soviets would take "reciprocal action." But whether they did or not, according to Nitze, America should proceed to scrap its own nuclear weapons.

The Nitze Asilomar Proposal was a plan to put 200,000,000 Americans at the mercy of the Soviets. If the Soviets built a Class A nuclear capability for themselves, then the U.S. would be left with no choice but surrender or nuclear destruction.

Nine months later, the new Kennedy-Johnson Administration took office. Nitze was immediately appointed Assistant Secretary of Defense, and men of his revolutionary views on defense swarmed into Government positions. In 1963 Nitze was promoted to Secretary of the Navy.

In 1967 Nitze became Deputy Secretary of Defense, the number-two man in the Pentagon. When McNamara was replaced as Secretary of Defense by Clark Clifford, it was generally understood in Washington that Clifford would be the "outside" or PR man whose principal duty would be to butter-up Congress and the news media, while Nitze would run the Pentagon. This was confirmed by *Newsweek* and *U.S. News & World Report*.

What Nitze urged "in the clear" in April 1960 has become an accomplished fact by 1968:

1. We have abandoned trying to achieve a true Class A nuclear capability, and

2. We have scrapped the weapons which made up our 1952-1962 Class A capability.

From Strength to Weakness

In January 1961 when the Eisenhower-Nixon Administration turned over control of the Federal Government to the newly-elected Kennedy-Johnson Administration, the United States had decisive military superiority over every other nation in the world. We enjoyed more than a 5-to-1 lead in nuclear striking power over our nearest rival, the Soviet Union. This great nuclear power was what saved America from disaster at the time of the Cuban Missile Crisis in 1962.

Since 1962, the United States has suffered a 50% decline in nuclear striking power, while the Soviets have increased theirs approximately 300%. The more than 5-to-1 lead in nuclear strength which the United States had over the Soviet Union is now completely gone, and our nation is in great and increasing peril.[6] The responsibility for this decline must be laid upon the Johnson Administration, upon Robert McNamara who was Secretary of Defense during the period when this drastic decline took place, and upon Paul Nitze who laid out the plan which McNamara followed.

In 1960, the principal issue used by John F. Kennedy in his Presidential campaign against Richard Nixon was the so-called "missile gap." There was no such thing as a missile gap. It was merely a figment of the imagination of Kennedy's speechwriters. After Kennedy was elected, his own Defense Department admitted that there never was any "missile gap."[7]

Let us look at the ten real and grave "gaps" in our nation's defenses which exist *now* after eight years of Robert McNamara and Paul Nitze.

1. The Megatonnage Gap

The most striking result of eight years of the McNamara policies is the megatonnage gap which now exists, and the massive megatonnage gap which will exist within the next three years if present policies are not reversed immediately.

"Megatonnage" is the word used to measure the firepower of nuclear weapons. "Megatonnage delivery capability" means how much nuclear firepower we can hit the enemy with. In the nuclear age, this is the most important measure of a nation's military strength.

The chart on the next page from the U.S. House Armed Services Committee Report of July 1967 entitled *The Changing Strategic Military Balance, U.S.A. vs. U.S.S.R.* shows that, in 1962 at the time of the Cuban Missile Crisis, we had at least a 5-to-1 lead over the Soviets in nuclear firepower. Since then, our nuclear strength has steadily decreased, while the Soviets have increased their nuclear firepower at a rapid rate. This chart proves that the Nitze proposal of 1960 to abandon our Class A nuclear capability was carried out during the McNamara-Nitze years.

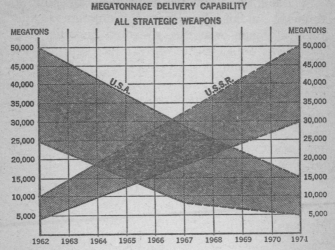

MEGATONNAGE DELIVERY CAPABILITY
ALL STRATEGIC WEAPONS

This chart also proves that the Soviets did not indulge in any "reciprocal action," but increased their nuclear arsenal as rapidly as they could. The year 1967 was the crossover year when the Soviets went ahead of the U.S. in megatonnage delivery capability. If present policies are continued, the Soviets will have a massive lead over us by 1971.

This graphic summary of what happened to the defense of America when it was entrusted to the stewardship of Robert McNamara was prepared by a distinguished committee which included General Bernard A. Schriever, chairman (longtime chief of our missile command), General Curtis LeMay (former Air Force Chief of Staff), General Thomas Power (former Commander-in-Chief of SAC who for 7 years was in charge of 90% of the Free World's firepower), General Albert Wedemeyer (author of the Wedemeyer Report), and Dr. Edward Teller (father of the H-bomb).

This chart illustrates that in 1962 our country was safe from the evil designs of any aggressor — but in 1968 our nation is increasingly at the mercy of the Soviets who have repeatedly boasted that they intend to bury us. Within the next couple of years, the Soviets will have the nuclear capability of doing exactly that — because the Nitze Proposal will have been carried out to the point where our only choice will be nuclear destruction or surrender. This chart proves that it wasn't any accident; it was planned that way.

2. The Delivery Vehicle Gap

When the Republican Administration left the White House in 1961, the United States was vastly superior to the Soviets in strategic nuclear delivery vehicles, which means the *vehicles* which can deliver nuclear weapons (such as missiles and bombers) on the enemy. During the McNamara Administration, our lead was lost because McNamara literally scrapped hundreds of delivery vehicles we had under the Eisenhower-Nixon Administration, and McNamara refused to build any new ones except for a reduced number of those already ordered by the Eisenhower Administration.

By 1967 the Soviets had gone ahead of the United States in strategic delivery vehicles, thus creating a gap which places our nation in great danger. The chart on the following page is from the report entitled *The Soviet Military Technological Challenge* published by the Georgetown University Center for Strategic Studies in September 1967, and prepared by Admiral Arleigh Burke, Lt. General Arthur Trudeau (former Army Chief of Research and Development), Dr. Harold Agnew (Weapons Development Leader, Los Ala-

TOTAL STRATEGIC DELIVERY VEHICLES

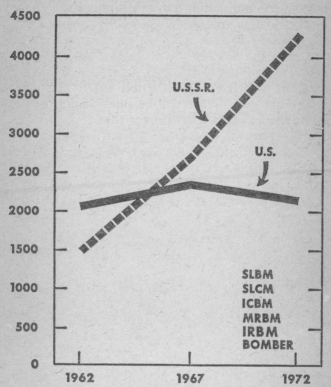

mos Scientific Laboratory), et al. Note how sharply
the U.S.S.R. is pulling ahead of us, and how fast
the gap will increase within the next few years
if the McNamara-Nitze policies are not reversed
at once.

The actual figures which went into this chart
are specified by one of the authorities at the
Georgetown Center for Strategic Studies, Dr.
James H. McBride, in the following from *U.S.
News & World Report* of February 26, 1968.

SOVIETS' MISSILE THREAT —
A DANGER FOR U. S.
TODAY: U. S. has 2,345 strategic nuclear delivery vehicles, U.S.S.R. has 2,700.

"Strategic nuclear delivery vehicles" include not only ICBMs — intercontinental ballistic missiles — and submarine-launched ballistic missiles, but submarine-based cruise missiles, strategic bombers and Soviet medium-range ballistic missiles.

BY 1972: U. S. will have 2,121 strategic nuclear delivery vehicles, U.S.S.R. will have 4,230.

Soviet arsenal in 1972 will include 1,780 ICBMs, against 1,000 U. S. Minuteman ICBMs, Dr. McBride reports. He adds: "The Soviet ICBM carries about 10 times the weight, or megatonnage, of the Minuteman, meaning that a Soviet ICBM may be able to carry at least six multiple, individually guided warheads, each capable of striking a different target with the explosive force equal to one Minuteman warhead. There is the strong possibility, therefore, that the Minuteman force of 1,000 missiles may be the equivalent of less than 200 Soviet ICBMs."

3. The Real Missile Gap

The first line of our nuclear missile defense is made up of the 1,000 Minuteman one-megaton missiles. This splendid weapon was developed and ordered under the Eisenhower-Nixon Administration. McNamara cut back the number of Minutemen originally planned from 2,000 to 1,200, and finally fixed the number at 1,000.[8]

McNamara scrapped 3/4 of our multi-megaton missiles — the so-called "big guns" in our nuclear arsenal. McNamara hired electricians and demolition men to deactivate 149 of our 203 multimegaton missiles and then he sold their launch silos. He destroyed all our Atlas and Titan I missiles, built at great cost; and before he left the Defense Department he announced plans for scrapping all the Titan II missiles. McNamara called them "obsolete," although each one was 7 times more powerful than each Minuteman.

This is precisely what Nitze called for when he said "scrap the fixed base vulnerable systems that have their principal utility as components of a Class A capability."

The present Administration has refused to build any missiles larger than the one-megaton Minuteman, and McNamara cancelled our most powerful weapon, the 24-megaton bomb.[9] Meanwhile, Soviet weapons average 10 megatons, and McNamara testified on August 13, 1963 that the Soviets have tested a "device" which could be "weaponized . . . at about a hundred megatons."[10]

During most of his Administration, Secretary McNamara argued that it didn't matter that the Soviet warheads were *bigger*, because the U.S. had *more* missiles. He left the Defense Department just in time to escape admitting that Soviet production of strategic nuclear missiles has increased so greatly that now they even have *more* missiles than we have, in addition to a monopoly on the bigger ones. Study the chart on the following page, taken from *The Soviet Military Technological Challenge*, which compares U.S. and U.S.S.R. missile production. It shows that our missile production has been at a standstill for two years, while the Soviets are adding 380 ICBMs a

COMPARISON OF
U.S. AND SOVIET MISSILE PRODUCTION

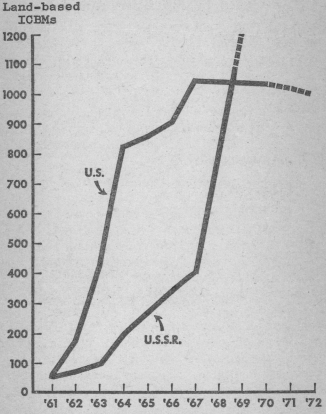

year. This is the real missile gap.

McNamara scrapped *all* U.S. intermediate and medium-range missiles, while the Soviets have 750 such missiles threatening NATO cities and bases. Nothing is left of the extremely expensive U.S. complex of Thor and Jupiter missiles installed in Turkey, Italy and England, which were capable of countering these Soviet missiles in Europe. This is shown by the following chart taken from *The Changing Strategic Military Balance, U.S.A. vs. U.S.S.R.* issued by the House Armed Services Committee.

IRBM/MRBM BALANCE
INTERMEDIATE/MEDIUM RANGE BALLISTIC MISSILES

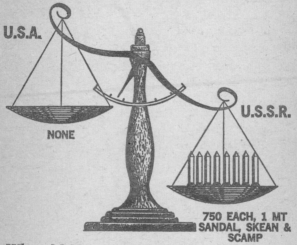

U.S.A.

NONE

U.S.S.R.

750 EACH, 1 MT
SANDAL, SKEAN &
SCAMP

When McNamara scrapped all our IRBM and MRBM missiles, he argued that they were "obsolete." The fact is, however, that they had hardly been installed when they were removed, and the Soviets did not scrap their IRBMs and MRBMs of the same type.

4. The Bomber Gap

When President Eisenhower left the White House, the United States had 2,710 strategic bombers, i.e., bombers capable of carrying nuclear weapons to the enemy.

During the last 7 years, McNamara scrapped 1,445 of these strategic bombers and also disarmed 600 carrier bombers of their strategic nuclear weapons. This means that McNamara did what no enemy could have done; he "took out" ¾ of our strategic nuclear bombers. Many of them today are rotting in the desert sun near Tucson.

The excuse given for scrapping the B-47s was that they are obsolete. But General Thomas Power, who headed our Strategic Air Command during the Cuban Missile Crisis, said: "I think the B-47 fleet in the hands of professionals could deliver weapons in the year 2000."[11]

We should not scrap planes until they are replaced with something better. This, McNamara did not do. He absolutely refused to build the B-70 or any advanced manned strategic bomber. He simply ordered a fantastic 75% reduction of our bomber force.

STRATEGIC NUCLEAR-ARMED BOMBERS

	Under Eisenhower	1968
B47s	1,400	0
B-52s	630	585
B58s	80	80
Carrier-based	600	0
	2,710	665*

*In his new book *The Essence of Security*, McNamara states that we now have only "about 600" strategic bombers.

On December 8, 1965 McNamara announced plans to scrap more than half (345) of the remaining B-52s, and all 80 B-58s, and replace them with 210 F-111s. Our 6,000 Marines who were surrounded at Khe Sanh can be grateful that this is one disarmament project which McNamara did not complete before he left the Defense Department. It was the precision bombing of the great B-52s which finally broke the siege of Khe Sanh and saved our brave Marines.

Within the last two hours of his tenure as Secretary of Defense, McNamara canceled what was still left of our "airborne alert." He did this *after* admitting that the new Soviet fractional orbital bomb (FOBS) could strike our bomber bases with zero warning. The SAC airborne alert was a brilliantly-conceived way to secure a powerful deterrent effect, without extra cost, by making use of the routine training flights of our strategic bombers. The cancellation of the airborne alert was craven appeasement of the Soviets and a severe blow to the defense of the United States.

5. The Anti-Missile Gap

One of the principal functions of the Federal Government, according to the U.S. Constitution, is to "provide for the common defense." The clearest case of the failure of the present Administration to provide for the common defense is its stubborn refusal to build any anti-missile system which can protect America from a Soviet nuclear attack.

For three years, the Joint Chiefs of Staff have unanimously and urgently recommended the building of an anti-missile system. For at least three years, the Soviets have been deploying their own anti-missile defense. Yet, the McNamara Whiz Kids gagged the Joint Chiefs and refused to permit the United States to erect any defenses against a missile attack. The result is the anti-missile gap which is pictured on the following page, clearly showing that the Soviets have this essential weapon and we have not.

Finally, in the face of Congressional demands for an anti-missile system, McNamara reluctantly

ABM BALANCE
ANTI-BALLISTIC MISSILE

U.S.A.

NONE
NIKE-X NOT DEPLOYED

U.S.S.R.

GALOSH, GRIFFON,
TALLINN SYSTEM

agreed in September 1967 to make a start on a "thin" anti-missile system which would protect us only against Red China in the 1970s, but would not protect our people or our missiles from a Soviet attack. This "thin" system was named the Sentinel. Clark Clifford made front-page headlines in September 1968 by announcing that he would "press forward" on the Sentinel. This is the same "thin," inadequate system McNamara agreed to — a full year earlier. The Sentinel has been subject to the same stall and delay that has doomed every new weapon for the last eight years.

The "thin" anti-missile is *not* what the Joint Chiefs recommend; they believe we must have a full anti-missile system to protect America from a *Soviet* nuclear attack today.

In addition to making the United States vulnerable to a *missile* attack, the civilians in the Pentagon have also rendered us vulnerable to a Soviet nuclear *bomber* attack. The present Administration quietly phased out most of our bomber defenses years before we can hope for new ones. Each year, McNamara rejected the military's unanimously request for new bomber defenses with the specious argument that, since we have no defense against missiles, little would be served by bomber defenses. High military sources have been quoted as saying that this is "another in a long series of 'calculated risks.'" Although we have developed a fine 2000-mile-an-hour bomber-interceptor plane (F-12), McNamara refused to produce it.

To make sure that America is completely defenseless, on August 16, 1968 the Pentagon closed down 23 anti-bomber missile batteries (called Nike-Hercules) capable of shooting down the fastest enemy bombers.

6. The Space Weapons Gap

The space weapon gap is shown by the chart on the next page from the report on *The Changing Strategic Military Balance, U.S.A. vs. U.S.S.R.* It makes clear that the U.S. has *no* space weapon whatsoever, while the Soviets have their 30-megaton weapon called the Scrag. This weapon has been repeatedly displayed in Moscow beginning in May 1965.

On November 3, 1967, Secretary McNamara announced at a press conference that the Soviets now have an orbital weapon called the FOBS which is capable of hurling nuclear warheads with zero warning on the United States from space in 1968.

SPACE WEAPON BALANCE

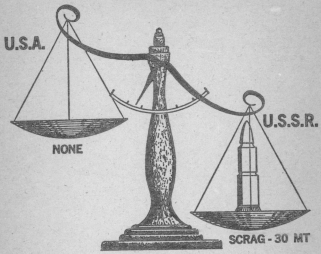

In his press conference, McNamara went on to say that the new Soviet orbital bomb would *not* violate the space treaty which we signed with the Soviets under the United Nations — because the Soviet orbital bomb is designed to hit its target *before* it makes a complete orbit, and only weapons which make one full orbit around the earth are considered to be "in space." This is one of the most appeasing statements ever made by a Secretary of Defense.

In other words, McNamara told the Soviets that we will not consider it a violation of the space treaty if their new orbital nuclear bomb (the FOBS) destroys U.S. cities — provided the bomb strikes the U.S. before it completes its first orbit. This craven interpretation of the space treaty was confirmed by the State Department.

The Associated Press reported on April 25,

1968 that it is believed that the Soviets are using their Cosmos satellite program as a "cover" for testing the FOBS. On August 28, 1968, the Soviets launched Cosmos 237.[12]

7. The Overseas Bases Gap

A base close to the enemy is one of the most important of all strategic advantages. When the Eisenhower-Nixon Administration left the White House, we had important missile and bomber bases close to Soviet borders. Secretary McNamara closed down all our strategic missile and bomber bases close to Russia, including those in Turkey, Italy, England, and North Africa. While McNamara was retreating from our Mediterranean bases the Soviets moved into the former French naval base of Mers-el-Kebir in Algeria, as well as into the former British bases, Alexandria and Port Said in Egypt. The Mediterranean used to be virtually an American lake, but now the Soviet Navy interferes with U.S. Navy maneuvers and even deliberately *bumps* our ships.

Also, the Soviets, in violation of the Monroe Doctrine, have built missile and submarine bases in Cuba, only 90 miles off our coast. The Soviets can use Cuba for electronic "terminal guidance" of their ICBMs to score direct hits on U.S. targets.

8. The Submarine Gap

The Soviet submarine fleet consists of about 350 conventional-powered and 50 nuclear-powered submarines, according to the Center for Strategic Studies report. In testimony released on July 4, 1968, Senator John Stennis, Chairman of the Senate Preparedness Investigation Subcommittee, said:

"The U.S. is substantially inferior to the Soviet

Union in terms of numbers of operational submarines."[13]

The same report quoted Vice Admiral Hyman G. Rickover as telling the Senators:

"I think if we work hard, we can try to catch up."

Soviet production of nuclear-powered missile-firing submarines continues at the rate of five or more per year. The U.S.S.R. has developed new nuclear-powered *attack* submarines for anti-submarine purposes. Typical are the new Leninsky-Komsomol hunter-killers which are fast, deep-diving attack submarines designed to shadow and destroy our Polaris submarines.

Vice Admiral Hyman G. Rickover testified in June 1968 that the Soviet submarine fleet is entirely post-World War II, while two-thirds of American attack submarines were built during World War II and are nearly 25 years old.

Despite Rickover's protests, McNamara refused to authorize the building of any new nuclear-propelled attack submarines, or any electric-driven silent submarines, to counter the large new Soviet attack submarine fleet. McNamara also refused to build any more missile-firing submarines and he froze the number of our Polaris submarines at 41. Admiral Rickover charged that the principal tactic used to delay submarine progress is "to study things to death."[14]

Almost all Soviet surface ships and many submarines are equipped with ship-to-ship or cruise missiles carrying conventional or nuclear warheads. The U.S. Navy is not equipped with any such missiles.

In a quarter-billion dollar blunder, McNamara refused to permit our latest carrier, the *John F. Kennedy*, to be nuclear powered. This was like building a new locomotive powered by an old-fashioned steam engine which requires frequent refueling.

9. The New Weapons Gap

American inventive genius has developed many new strategic weapons which could play an important part in the defense of America in the nuclear age. The Eisenhower-Nixon Administration invested millions of dollars in the development of new weapons, believing that the United States must stay ahead, scientifically and technologically.

The present Administration has refused to produce any new weapon system, and has canceled or stalled many that the Eisenhower Administration started, including Skybolt, Pluto, Dynasoar and Orion.[15]

One of the techniques developed in recent years to protect a nation's missiles from being destroyed by the enemy is "mobility." A moving target is obviously much harder to hit than a stationary one. All our land-based missiles are in fixed locations, well known to the enemy. Many Soviet missiles are known to be mobile.

Our Strategic Air Command developed a plan to equip each of 60 moving trains with five Minuteman launchers and crews. After the Eisenhower-Nixon Administration spent $108,000,000 perfecting the mobile Minuteman program, McNamara vetoed it on December 13, 1961.[16]

The Navy developed a plan to ensure mobility of MRBMs by putting them on surface ships. McNamara vetoed this.

On July 7, 1968 the Senate Preparedness Investigating Subcommittee made public recent testimony of General Earle G. Wheeler, Chairman of the Joint Chiefs. General Wheeler listed the following measures recommended by the Joint Chiefs for the 1969 budget which were all vetoed by McNamara:[17]

1) Full-scale development of a new, supersized ICBM.

2) A prototype of a new ballistic-missile ship.

3) Air-to-ground missiles for late-model B52s.

4) Full development of an advanced strategic bomber.

5) Further improvement of Polaris A-3 missile system.

6) Deployment of Nike X anti-missile defense for cities.

7) Production of F-12 jet interceptors.

10. The Nuclear Technology Gap

On August 15, 1963 the Joint Chiefs of Staff told the Senate Foreign Relations Committee: "The U.S.S.R. is ahead of the United States in the high-yield (tens of megatons) technology, in weapons-effect knowledge derived from high-yield explosives, and in the yield/weight ratios of high-yield devices."[18]

The House Armed Services Committee report on *The Changing Strategic Military Balance* concluded: "Thus it would appear that since 1961, the Soviets have had a 5-to-1 advantage over the U.S. in yield/weight ratio in contrast to their pre-1961 inferiority."

What this means is that, if both countries use their best weapons, Soviet strategic bombers can deliver $2\frac{1}{2}$ times more megatons than U.S. bombers. This is one part of the nuclear technology gap.

Another part of the nuclear technology gap is the Soviet superior knowledge and use of the X-ray effect. The X-ray concept "is that in the vacuum of space a thermonuclear explosion gives off most of its energy in the form of highly energetic X-rays that can travel hundreds of miles with the speed of light. If these X-rays impinge on an object, such as a warhead, their energy is translated quickly into heat." When used in an anti-missile system, the X-ray effect thus destroys incoming missiles in space by an "area defense" without having to score direct or near-direct hits.

The Soviets conducted four times as many high-yield tests in space as we did, and this is how they discovered the X-ray effect which can literally shield a country from enemy missiles.

TFX — The Flying Edsel

Every nuclear weapon which defends our country today was built or developed under the Eisenhower Administration.

The *only* new strategic weapon which was produced during the 8 years of the present Administration is the TFX plane, later christened the F-111, but often referred to as the Flying Edsel.

The contract to build the TFX plane was the largest contract in the history of Federal spending. Every evaluation board in the Pentagon recommended the bid of the Boeing Company as a better plane at a lower price. But McNamara and his political aides overruled them and awarded the contract instead to General Dynamics which promised to make the plane in Texas (whereas the Boeing plane would have been made in Kansas).[19]

The price tag which was originally $6.5 billion has doubled; it is now $13 billion, and this is for 400 fewer planes. Production is three years behind schedule, and the plane has been constantly plagued by technical difficulties. Eight F-111s have crashed because of what the Pentagon called "in-flight emergencies." The F-111s sent to Vietnam were not used in combat with MIGs; three crashed in Laos and Thailand.[20] On September 6, 1968, the *Washington Post* reported a new structural failure in the center section where the wings pivot, and cancellation of plans to send the F-111 into combat.

The Navy version is now admitted by everyone to be a total failure, unfit for use. The Senate killed it on March 29 by refusing to appropriate one more dollar for it. The Pentagon buried it on July 10 when it announced final cancellation. This means at least one billion dollars down the TFX drain, and now the Navy is calling for new bids to start all over again.

The TFX is a sordid tale of corrupt politics and conflicts of interest beyond anything ever before seen in the United States. Two high Defense Department civilians received financial favors from the corporation to which they awarded the contract, namely, General Dynamics.

But that is not all. Whereas the TFX decision *appeared* to be the result of McNamara's incompetence, bad judgment and stupidity, it actually was his most deceptive accomplishment in carrying out the Nitze proposal to reduce U.S. nuclear striking power. How?

1) While billions of dollars were diverted down the TFX drain, we have not bought the weapons we need for the defense of America, such as more advanced ICBMs, the anti-missile, and advanced interceptors to defend against a Soviet bomber attack.

2) By holding out the F-111 bomber version as a substitute for a true strategic bomber, McNamara

delayed for years the development of the advanced manned strategic aircraft which we so urgently need.

3) McNamara knew in advance that, even if the TFX did everything he claimed, it would be obsolete as a tactical fighter before it was built. The U.S.S.R. has already produced a swing-wing fighter plane and new model MIGs which are so much faster that the TFX is no longer even classified as a fighter plane.

It Was Planned That Way

When Paul Nitze in 1960 laid out his plan of abandoning our Class A nuclear capability, he said he "hoped" the Soviets would follow suit with reciprocal action. Although the U.S. scrapped 50% of its nuclear strength and declined to build the new weapons we had developed, the historical record is clear that the Soviets did *not* take one single reciprocal action. On July 8, 1968, Brezhnev taunted the United States:

"As long as imperialism exists . . . the Socialist countries will strengthen their defenses in every way."

Nobody but a fool could have believed in 1960 that the Soviets would reciprocate. And Nitze and McNamara are not fools.

When it became apparent — after one year, after two years, after three years, after four years, after five years, after six years, after seven years — that the Soviets were actually *increasing* their nuclear arsenal at a rapid rate, *why didn't the Nitze-McNamara policy change?*

There is only one realistic answer. Obviously, Nitze and McNamara deliberately meant to *reduce* U.S. nuclear strength at the same time they knew that Soviet power was rapidly growing.

Mao Tse-tung taught that "all political power comes out of the barrel of a gun." The nuclear-age version of this is: All political power comes out of the nuclear weapon. This means that the day is rapidly approaching when the only alternatives facing the United States will be (1) surrender to the Soviets or (2) nuclear destruction.

Does that mean that these men must be Communists? No. They are simply men who have secretly decided that they would rather be Red than even *risk* being dead, and that therefore surrender to the Soviets is not only preferable to nuclear war, but is even preferable to being *able* to resist a Soviet ultimatum. And the only way to make sure that their plan to surrender us is not goofed up by American patriots who would rather risk a fight or a confrontation than be Red — is to make the U.S. *so much weaker* than the Soviets that resistance will be as hopeless as the poor Czechs shaking their fists at the Soviet tanks.

In anti-trust cases, the U.S. courts have held that what is called "consciously parallel business behavior" is evidence of a conspiracy.[21] In order to prove a conspiracy to monopolize, the Government does not have to show that corporate officers actually met together in some smoke-filled room and conspired to restrict trade. The corporate officers may be convicted by the public evidence of their taking action which was consciously parallel to what others were doing to restrict competition.

Likewise, the consciously-parallel behavior of Pentagon civilians such as McNamara, Nitze, Roswell Gilpatric, and Harold Brown, to reduce U.S. military strength and to appease the Soviet Union, is evidence that they truly, in Lincoln's words, "worked upon a common plan."

chapter VII

THE LIVING LIE

> "Oh, what a tangled web we weave,
> When first we practice to deceive!"

The second technique by which slick men conceal their true objectives is the weaving of a web of lies as a "cover" for their subversive or "extracurricular" activities.

Any reader of advice-to-the-lovelorn columns knows the web of fabrication spun by the philandering husband to his girl friend: "My wife doesn't understand me; she is cold and indifferent; we're only staying together until the children are grown; then I will marry you, but meanwhile . . ." The same tired-out line continues to deceive young women — especially those who do not want to recognize it as simply a tissue of lies invented and embellished to attain a desired objective.

When Franklin D. Roosevelt was a candidate for President in 1932, he made these solemn promises to the American people:

"I shall . . . reduce the cost of the current Federal Government operations by 25%."[1]

"Let us have the courage to stop borrowing to meet continuing deficits. Stop the deficits."[2]

"I propose . . . to discuss up and down the country, in all seasons and at all times, the duty of reducing taxes. . . . Nothing I have said in this campaign transcends in importance this covenant with the taxpayers of this country."[3]

It should be clear to everyone now that Roose-

velt's promises to reduce Federal spending by
25%, balance the budget, and reduce taxes were
nothing but a "cover" to camouflage the revolutionary economic changes his New Deal would
bring to Washington.

Probably the Communists have spun the largest and most variegated web of lies to disguise
their nefarious designs. All their palaver about
the "state withering away," "social reform," and
"to each according to his needs," is designed (1)
to entrap dupes and do-gooders, and (2) to provide a layer of protective covering under which
the Reds can operate. Those who really believe
the so-called Communist "philosophy" are considered to be of too limited intelligence to rise
very high in the Communist apparatus.

Colonel Oleg Penkovskiy, the highest ranking
Communist in recent years to renounce Communism, a brave man who worked inside the
Kremlin while sending documents to the West,
made it clear in his writings that all that so-called
"philosophy" is really just a device to achieve
power over men and nations. In his book *The
Penkovskiy Papers* he said:

> "My eyes were opened by my work with the
> higher authorities and general officers of the So-
> viet Army. I happened to marry a general's
> daughter and I quickly found myself in a society
> of the Soviet upper classes. I realized that their
> praise of the Party and Communism was only in
> words. . . . Our Communism, which we now have
> been building for almost 45 years, is a fraud.[4] . . .
> *"Among my friends, Party members of today,
> there is none that believes in Communism."*[5]
> (emphasis added)

In the same way, the betrayers have spun a
web as a "cover" for their plan to surrender

America. It is a tangled web which includes all the false liberal notions about Communism which anti-Communists much-too-tolerantly refer to as "fallacies" or "errors." These are:

1) Communism is "mellowing." (In his State of the Union Address, President Johnson said we should "build bridges" to Communist countries and seek an "accommodation" with them.)

2) The Soviets want "peaceful coexistence" and "peaceful competition." (Shortly before the 1968 invasion of Czechoslovakia, Hubert Humphrey said we must "shift from policies of confrontation and containment to policies of reconciliation and peaceful engagement.")

3) Communism is no longer "monolithic" and the satellites are developing some degree of freedom. (Only a few days before the invasion of Czechoslovakia, Hubert Humphrey stated that the Eastern European nations are now "relatively autonomous.")

4) The new Soviet leaders are really businessmen in "gray-flannel suits" — not tyrants like Stalin. (On July 4, 1968, *The New York Times* printed a profile on Brezhnev entitled "Red in Gray Flannel.")

5) We should rely on "negotiations" and agreements with the Soviet Union.

No one who knows anything of the historical record of Communism for the last 30 years could possibly believe those foolish fairy tales. They are disproved by the Korean War, the butchery of Budapest, the Berlin Wall, the nuclear missiles sent into Cuba, the Vietnam War, and the 1968 Soviet invasion of Czechoslovakia. The Senate Internal Security Subcommittee documented more than 100 treaty violations by the Soviet Union.

Why, then, do the gravediggers, presumably intelligent men, still talk as though they believe these incredible falsehoods? Obviously, because it serves their purposes. It entraps the dupes and it diverts into intellectual blind alleys all those who seek to unmask the betrayal at the top. It keeps informed anti-Communists busy refuting falsehoods which the gravediggers don't believe anyway — instead of facing up to the unpleasant truth of *why* the gravediggers make statements they obviously could not believe.

Robert McNamara is no longer Secretary of Defense. Why, then, should he still concern us? There are at least three compelling reasons.

1. McNamara's policies still dominate and frustrate the defense of the United States. Clark Clifford has made no change in the McNamara policies except, reluctantly and under protest, to cancel the Navy TFX plane, which he did only after Congress refused to appropriate any more money for it and there was no alternative. The Associated Press reported on August 29, 1968:

> "Clifford also has kept virtually intact the team of civilian analysts, administrators and aides McNamara assembled in the office of Secretary of Defense."

The McNamara policies still stand in the way of a swift and victorious end of the war in Vietnam. The McNamara policies still permit the Soviets to follow up their invasion of Czechoslovakia with a nuclear blackmail threat to the United States.

2. McNamara exercised more power, and produced more potentially disastrous results than any man in the history of the world. He spent more

money — more than $400,000,000,000.00 — with more autocratic control over it than any man in history. Yet, in spending so much money, he managed to reduce by more than 50% the strategic military power of the United States. If you and your family are incinerated by a hydrogen holocaust, McNamara is the man who made this possible and probable. If we are forced to surrender under the threat of such a strike — and you and your children are, like the Czechs, helpless to do anything except shake your fists at the Soviet Army of occupation — McNamara is the man most responsible. He said he would like to be known as the "Secretary of Peace." He did not name the price of the peace he was trying to buy. The price of peace with the Soviets is always surrender. Perhaps surrender on the installment plan; perhaps a camouflaged or face-saving surrender, if the masters of the Kremlin are magnanimous; but always the final price is surrender.

3. The American people, the new Congress, and especially the new Administration, must understand what McNamara and the LBJ Administration have done to the defense of the United States. Otherwise, it can never be undone in time to avert disaster. The invasion of Czechoslovakia may be our last timely warning.

In the previous chapter we examined how McNamara carried out the Nitze disarmament policies and exactly how McNamara scrapped more than half the strategic nuclear strength of the United States. Now let us examine the technique by which he covered his tracks: the tangled web of outright lies he has spun to conceal the damage he has wrought and to confuse those who seek to refute him.

The Essence of McNamaraism

In late August 1968, McNamara published a new book called *The Essence of Security* which was obviously planned to serve as his "valedictory" and his self-justification for his 7 years as Secretary of Defense. The book is a skein of sophisticated lies to camouflage his implementation of the Nitze proposal to reduce the nuclear strength of the U.S. so disastrously that we will be forced to surrender because fighting will be hopeless.

One of the leading book review journals immediately published a feature review of McNamara's book by former Secretary of State Dean Acheson.[6] Acheson began his adulatory review by comparing McNamara to General George Marshall. Acheson meant his comparison as an accolade for McNamara — but the comparison is far more apt than Acheson realized.

General George Marshall is the one primarily responsible for the surrender of China to Communism. He foolishly took Owen Lattimore's advice and signed the Republic of China's death warrant by cutting off "all arms and ammunition supplies to China in 1946-47 in order to force Chiang Kai-shek to come to terms with the Communists."[7] In Marshall's own words,

"As Chief of Staff I armed 39 anti-Communist divisions, now with a stroke of the pen I disarm them."

Robert McNamara is the one primarily responsible for the disarmament of U.S. nuclear weapons which, unless quickly reversed, will mean the surrender of America to Soviet Communism.

After the truth about our State Department's sellout of China was exposed in the U.S. Senate,

Senator William Jenner labeled Marshall "a living lie." Now there is another high U.S. official more deserving of the title of "a living lie" — Robert S. McNamara.

After echoing the worn-out liberal cliches such as "collective security," "accommodation with the Soviet Union," the end of "monolithic" Communism, "building bridges," "peaceful competition" with the Communists, and the hope for "agreements" with the Soviets, and after acknowledging his "debt" to Paul Nitze, Roswell Gilpatric (who resigned as Deputy Secretary of Defense after Senate hearings documented his receipt of large sums of money from the corporation to which he helped give the TFX contract), Arthur Sylvester (best known for his infamous line "the government has the right to lie"), Harold Brown (the principal hatchet man in charge of scrapping new weapons), Adam Yarmolinsky, and others, McNamara in his new book proceeds to build his case around the following lies. It should be remembered that McNamara is *not* a scientist, and *not* a military man — he is an accountant who, on strategic matters, can't, or won't, count correctly.

1. McNamara: "It is now impossible for either the United States or the Soviet Union to achieve a meaningful victory over the other in a strategic nuclear exchange."[8]

This is false. McNamara's own official statements to Congress concede that the Soviets can kill 150,000,000 Americans, or 75% of our people, in a surprise attack — but we can only kill a maximum of 33% of Russians. McNamara can't count. This would certainly be a "meaningful" victory for the Soviets. Furthermore, competent authorities have shown that McNamara's figure of

33% is falsely inflated by at least one half.[9]

2. McNamara: We have "assured-destruction capability . . . a highly reliable ability to inflict unacceptable damage upon any single aggressor or combination of aggressors . . . even after absorbing a surprise first strike."[10]

This is false. We have no such "assured-destruction capability." We have no assurance that we will have enough functioning missiles "after absorbing a surprise first strike" to penetrate Soviet anti-missile defenses and destroy vital targets.

Our Polaris submarines are shadowed by Soviet killer subs and may be knocked out as quietly and mysteriously as was the Scorpion. It is even more probable that Soviet missiles can destroy our Polaris submarines after they launch their first missile. Our submarines cannot fire a salvo of their 16 missiles; there must be an interval between each firing. Even though fired from underwater, the Polaris missile can be detected by Soviet radar and satellite intelligence as soon as its rocket ignites as it rises above the ocean surface. With instant-action computers, the Soviets can immediately launch their missiles at the submarine.

Our land-based missiles, all in fixed locations well-known to the enemy, are even more vulnerable. The electromagnetic pulse from Soviet multi-megaton warheads may prevent *all* our land-based missiles from launching, or damage their guidance or firing mechanisms. Furthermore, we have no assurance whatsoever that they will not be duds, even if undamaged by Soviet weapons. The Minuteman missile has never had an operational test. On August 14, 1968, an attempted test of a Minuteman II missile in Michigan, North

Dakota, resulted in total failure — the giant ICBM failed to move from its silo when controls were activated.[11] Even if the launching were successful, we have no assurance that our missiles will function properly. In late summer 1967, some 40% of the Minuteman IIs were reported to be "not operational or not on alert because of malfunctions, leaving the nation comparatively naked to Communist ICBM attack."[12]

3. McNamara: "Is the Soviet Union seriously attempting to acquire a first-strike capability against the United States? . . . we believe the answer is no."[13]

This is false. A "first-strike" capability means an "anti-weapon" capability — the ability to knock out the enemy's weapons. For years, the Soviets have concentrated on building *multi*-megaton weapons especially designed to knock out our one-megaton Minuteman. In 1961-1962 the Soviets conducted a series of nuclear tests in the atmosphere which revealed their superior knowledge and arsenal of giant nuclear weapons. McNamara testified that the Soviets tested one "device" which would "weaponize" at 100-megatons.[14] In 1963, the U.S. Joint Chiefs of Staff testified that "the U.S.S.R. is ahead of the United States in the high-yield (tens of megatons) technology."[15] Nothing could be clearer proof of a "serious" attempt by the Soviets to acquire a first-strike (or anti-weapon) capability.

4. McNamara: "The most frequent question that arises . . . is whether or not the United States possesses nuclear superiority over the Soviet Union. The answer is that we do. . . . By both these standards [gross megatonnage and number of missile launchers] the United States does have

a substantial superiority over the Soviet Union."[16]

This is false. Read the proof in the Megatonnage Chart on page 53 and the Strategic Delivery Vehicles Chart on page 55.

5. McNamara: "None of the [anti-missile] systems at the present or foreseeable state of the art would provide an impenetrable shield over the United States."[17]

This is completely misleading. Note the weasel word "impenetrable." The excellent team of scientists under General Arthur Betts made exhaustive tests of the Nike X anti-missile and concluded that it would provide effective protection of Americans from nuclear attack. The U.S. Joint Chiefs of Staff for three years have unanimously and urgently recommended the building of the Nike X anti-missile.[18] A defensive weapon does not need to be "impenetrable" in order to be effective and necessary.

6. McNamara: "Were we to deploy a heavy ABM [anti-ballistic missile] system throughout the United States, the Soviets would clearly be strongly motivated to so increase their offensive capability as to cancel out our defensive advantage."[19]

This is completely false. The Soviets are *already* increasing their offensive capability as fast as they can. Read the proof on the Missile Production Chart on page 58. General Bernard Schriever, who directed this development and deployment of the Minuteman, said that Soviet "development and deployment of an advanced ABM system and testing of so-called 'global rockets' are clearly not in response to any similar U.S. efforts to date. . . . The Soviet Union is seeking technological and military superiority by pursuing any and all research and development efforts that will help them towards this goal — regardless of what we are doing."[20]

7. McNamara: "I would judge that a capability on our part to destroy, say, $\frac{1}{5}$ to $\frac{1}{4}$ of her [Soviet] population and $\frac{1}{2}$ of her industrial capacity would serve as an effective deterrent."[21]

This is false. The Russians entered World War II as a second-rate power which had difficulty defeating little Finland. Hitler inflicted almost this much damage on the Soviets, yet they emerged from World War II a first-rate power, able to move quickly and decisively into a dozen countries in Eastern Europe. The threat of losing $\frac{1}{5}$ to $\frac{1}{4}$ of the Soviet slave population would absolutely *not* deter the power-hungry men in the Kremlin from their goal of world conquest. It should be remembered that the Soviets deliberately starved 7 million of their own people just because they did not fit into the Soviet system of agriculture.[22]

8. McNamara: "The most likely kind of conflict in NATO Europe is one arising from miscalculation during a period of tension, rather than a deliberately preplanned Soviet attack."[23]

This is false. Every Soviet "conflict" has been a deliberately preplanned attack, including the Soviet attacks on Finland, Poland, Hungary, and Czechoslovakia. The Communists don't "miscalculate" — they "preplan" everything. General Martin Dzur, Czech Defense Minister, estimated that the 1968 invasion required at least six months to organize and prepare logistically.[24]

9. McNamara: "The root of man's security does not lie in his weaponry, it lies in his mind."[25]

This is false. Security from Hitler and Tojo did not lie in anybody's mind — it lay in bullets, bombs, torpedoes, B-17s, B-29s, radar, the proximity fuze, an expeditionary force of several million GIs, and the atom bomb. Security against the Soviets does not lie in treaties or pious hopes — it lies in nuclear weapons and anti-missiles, planes and submarines, and a Secretary of Defense who makes sure we have better weapons than any enemy.

McNamara devotes the last third of his book to expounding the liberal dogma on poverty, social injustice, open housing, the peace corps, etc., which have no relevance to the job of Secretary of Defense, but keep the liberals grinding out extravagant praise about his "computer" brain. A good clue to the type of bureaucrat he really is may be gleaned from this sentence:

"The real threat to democracy comes not from overmanagement but from undermanagement."[26]

The United States will be lucky to survive his overmanagement of our Department of Defense.

Any reasonably intelligent American can expose the lies and contradictions in McNamara's books and public statements. On logic and fact, McNamara scores zero — but on fluency with words to "cover" his destruction of U.S. nuclear superiority, he is the champion. These words of Joseph Addison can be appropriately applied to Robert McNamara:

"Is there not some chosen curse,
　Some hidden thunder in the stores of heaven,
　Red with uncommon wrath, to blast the man
　Who owes his greatness to his country's ruin?"

chapter VIII

THE MYTH OF THE MIRVs

Events began closing in on Robert McNamara in the summer of 1967. The activating power in his exposure was the House Armed Services Committee, despite its heavy Democratic majority. A year before, this Committee had issued a Report which charged that McNamara had deliberately deceived the Congress, usurped the authority of Congress, tried to obstruct Congressional committees in the performance of their duties, deliberately altered official testimony of the Joint Chiefs of Staff, and declared documents secret in order to protect his own position.[1] This Committee Report provided ample evidence for impeachment.

In July 1967 the House Armed Services Committee again put patriotism above politics and published the document (described in Chapter VI) called *The Changing Strategic Military Balance: U.S.A. vs. U.S.S.R.*, written by nationally-known military experts. This Report broke the logjam of lies which had so long "covered" McNamara and it revealed the true picture of what he had done to our strategic defenses.

Once the logjam was broken, additional evidence from many authoritative sources provided conclusive proof that McNamara's policies have brought about the scrapping of at least half of America's great nuclear striking power. The case against McNamara was so clear that the American businessman and housewife could understand it as well as the experts.

McNamara could no longer deny that the Soviets had caught up and were about to pass us in the number of missiles, or that they were already far ahead of us in the explosive power of their weapons, both individually and in total. He was forced into the position where he had to create some new basis for defending himself against the awful truth.

At the same time, McNamara was in dire need of an alibi to explain the great buildup of Soviet offensive forces and their extensive deployment of anti-missile defenses against the United States. McNamara had carefully concealed these facts from the American public for years, but now he had to answer such obvious questions from Congressmen and reporters as:

Mr. McNamara, if we needed 1,710 missiles to deter a Soviet attack *before* they deployed their anti-missile defense, don't we need many more now because some of our missiles will never reach their targets? What are you doing to protect the United States from the Soviet missiles which have *doubled* in number in the last two years?

McNamara was forced to provide plausible answers to these questions because a failure to do so would (1) open up a major campaign issue for 1968, and (2) strip the remaining "cover" from the damage his policies have done to U.S. defenses.

McNamara Midwifes the MIRV

McNamara's solution to his dilemma was his crowning masterpiece of 7 years of ultra-sophisticated deceit.

For years, McNamara had claimed that U.S. superiority over the Soviets rested on the *numbers* of our *missiles*. Now that he was faced with the fact that the Soviets had equaled the U.S. in numbers of missiles, McNamara shifted his ground and claimed that true superiority must be based instead on the number of *warheads*. By conjuring up great numbers of warheads, he could accomplish two things: (1) go back to his old numbers game and claim we have "superiority" over the Soviets, and (2) downgrade the importance of the Soviet anti-missile system by claiming we have enough warheads to saturate it.

The answer was McNamara's marvelous MIRV — Multiple Independently-Targeted Reentry Vehicle. He would *not* add a single missile or missile-launcher to U.S. operational forces, but he would subdivide the *warheads* on our *present* missiles into 3 to 10 little warheads.

The MIRV was a magician's trick to divide what we have and make it appear like more. Figures can't lie, but liars can figure. The creation of the MIRV was the same kind of "numbers racket" by which McNamara had earlier claimed "a 45% increase in the number of combat-ready Army divisions" by the simple device of re-dividing manpower and creating new divisions out of the troops we already had.[2]

McNamara's MIRV was so glamorous and exciting that he pulled a snow job on the entire press and public. One news magazine proclaimed that the MIRV program would "increase the number of ICBM warheads in the U.S. inventory from 1,710 to almost 7,500." A wire service upped this estimate to "a mind-staggering 8,000 to 16,000 warheads." Columnists and the public applauded.

No one seemed to care what was in the warheads, just so they were warheads. Few noted that we don't have them now anyway and it will take many years to get them.

What is a MIRV? The nose cone on a MIRV missile is, for practical purposes, a mother space ship which carries inside a brood of smaller space ships. The number can range from an anticipated 3 in Minuteman III, to 10 in Poseidon. By the mere fact of dividing the explosive into several smaller warheads, there will be at least a 40% loss of efficiency. In addition, each little space ship, or MIRV warhead, must have its own re-entry shield, its own shielding against X-ray effects and radiation, its own terminal guidance system, its own explosive material, its own fission trigger, and probably its own penetration aids and source of propulsion to permit it to change course. In the present Minuteman warheads, the payload is devoted mostly to explosive. In the MIRVs, the payload will have to make way for all the necessities of highly complex guidance, etc.

Paul Nitze, Deputy Secretary of Defense, in a debate with Congressman Craig Hosmer, senior Republican member of the Congressional Joint Committee on Atomic Energy, suggested that, when a 10-megaton single warhead (10,000,000 tons) is divided into 10 MIRVs, each MIRV warhead would have a yield of 50 kilotons (50,000 tons). Thus, each MIRV would have only $\frac{1}{2}$ of 1% of the original warhead power, and all 10 MIRVs together would have only 5% of the original warhead power. However, we have no missiles capable of carrying 10 megatons except 54 Titan II missiles which McNamara has scheduled for scrapping.

The largest single warhead we will have in the 1970s is the Poseidon which *at most* can carry a 3-megaton single warhead. Therefore, using Nitze's ratio, the MIRVs in the Poseidon would each be in the range of 15 to 20 kilotons, which is approximately the power of the Hiroshima bomb. Thus, instead of carrying 3,000,000 tons of TNT-explosive equivalent, the Poseidon would be reduced to carrying only 150,000 to 200,000 tons.

Turning Back The Clock

The MIRV was the perfect climax to all the disarmament programs McNamara had masterminded in his Pentagon career. Here is the way he described his MIRV program: "MIRVs will multiply the number of U.S. warheads by 10." But, when we "tell it like it is," based on Nitze's own figures, here is the result:

1) MIRVs will reduce the explosive power of *each* U.S. warhead by 99%.

2) MIRVs will reduce the explosive power of the total missile by 95%.

3) MIRVs will bring about the final liquidation of U.S. strategic nuclear power. It took McNamara 7 years to bring U.S. nuclear striking power down by more than 50%, and continuation of his already-announced programs will nosedive it to a 90% cut by 1972. Now, in a single new program, he will cut that remaining 10% capability by more than half — probably by 90%.

If McNamara's program of replacing our existing missiles with MIRVs goes ahead, he will have turned back the clock of U.S. nuclear power at least 10 years. The power of our weapons will be cut from the *megaton* range (millions of tons of

TNT-explosive equivalent) to the *kiloton* range (mere thousands of tons of TNT-explosive equivalent). The explosive power in the MIRV warheads will still be hydrogen (tritium-deuteride) produced — but the yield will be in the range of the primitive Hiroshima A-bomb rather than the H-super-bomb.

At the end of World War II, our development of the H-bomb was deliberately stalled for 5 years by persons who did not want the U.S. ever to be capable of using it against the Soviet Union. Whereas our H-bomb could have been ready in 1947, we did not have it until 1952, and then only because of the courage and genius of Dr. Edward Teller. The man principally responsible for the 5-year slowdown was J. Robert Oppenheimer, whose security clearance was finally revoked by the Atomic Energy Commission in 1954 — after he had done his damage.

Why did Oppenheimer do this and how did he get by with it for so long? He was a Dr. Jeckyll and Mr. Hyde who "by day" was director of the Los Alamos Laboratory, and "by night" was "contributing substantial monthly sums to the Communist Party; . . . had at least one Communist mistress; . . . and was in frequent contact with Soviet espionage agents."[3] He admitted that he told a "tissue of lies" when officially questioned about his contact with a Soviet agent.

If McNamara's MIRV program goes into effect, he will have done far more than Oppenheimer to prevent us from having the H-bomb for the protection of the American people.

The following stark word-picture was written by Andrei D. Sakharov, the father of the Soviet

H-bomb, as translated by *The New York Times*:

"Today one can consider a 3-megaton nuclear warhead as 'typical.' The area of fires from the explosion of such a warhead is 150 times greater than from the Hiroshima bomb and the area of destruction is 30 times greater. The detonation of such a warhead over a city would create a 100-square kilometer (40-square mile) area of total destruction and fire.

"Tens of millions of people would perish under the ruins of buildings, from fire and radiation, suffocate in the dust and smoke or die in shelters buried under debris. In the event of a ground-level explosion, the fallout of radioactive dust would create a danger of fatal exposure in an area of tens of thousands of kilometers."[4]

It just happens that 3 megatons is about the power of the warhead the Poscidon could deliver in a single package, whereas after the Poseidon is split into 10 MIRVs (with separate guidance systems, etc.) each warhead will have almost exactly the power of the Hiroshima bomb.

Furthermore, the high-yield, or larger, weapons have some effects which are lost completely in the low-yield weapons, including X-ray and electromagnetic pulse effects which disrupt communications and radar, and neutron effects. Just as a tank may be invulnerable to an infinite volume of rifle and machine-gun fire, but vulnerable to larger shells, so many Soviet targets (such as hardened missiles in underground silos, vital storage areas, communication facilities, and the Moscow subway shelter) are substantially invulnerable to low-yield weapons, but *are* vulnerable to high-yield multi-megaton weapons.

This is not to say that MIRV warheads do not have a valuable place in a mixed and balanced offensive missile force. They do. But only if *added* to our existing forces. If they are merely a substitute for the missiles we now have, the MIRVs will literally liquidate U.S. megatonnage delivery capability by missiles.

There is nothing — absolutely nothing — that MIRVs can do to improve our strategic missile position that cannot be done better *and sooner* by doubling the number of Minuteman missiles and by building *new* submarines for Poseidon missiles instead of substituting them on the Polaris submarines. It would be cheaper to build another 1,000 Minutemen than to replace our present 1,000 with MIRVs. McNamara admitted that the cost of rebuilding the Polaris submarines in order to equip them with Poseidon missiles would be at least 60% the cost of building an entire fleet of new submarines for the Poseidon missiles.

If we replace our present 1,000 Minutemen with MIRVs, the Soviets will still have only 1,000 targets to knock out. Each missile site they hit would knock out 3 warheads. If we take the cheaper and faster course of adding another 1,000 Minutemen, we would double the number of targets the Soviets would have to cover, and thereby double the survivability of our weapons in case of a Soviet attack.

The claim that MIRVs can saturate the Soviet anti-missile system better than single-warhead missiles is based entirely on the theory that the Soviet anti-missile system can only knock out incoming warheads one-by-one. There is no verification for this. On the contrary, their system seems designed to knock out incoming warheads while they are still out in space. In outer space, the X-ray effects travel great distances almost instantaneously, and thus give an "area defense" by knocking out the incoming MIRVs *before* they separate from the mother ship.

When Nitze claims that the MIRVs can destroy 10 times as many airfields and "soft" missile sites, he is literally targeting "empty holes." Obviously, since the Soviets will launch their attack first, their bombers and missiles will have "flown" from their bases before the U.S. could retaliate.

The Here And Now

McNamara and the press talk glibly about the MIRVs as though we have them in operation now! This is absolutely false. The U.S. MIRV system cannot possibly be ready in operational numbers until well into the 1970s.

The guidance problem for the MIRVs will take years to solve before it is a reliable operational system. In 1967, when 40% of the Minuteman II missiles were reported *not* operational or *not* on alert, the Secretary of the Air Force confessed that guidance problems were the cause. If we have so much trouble with the guidance of single-warhead missiles, with 10 years of design and production experience behind them, what can we expect of the tremendously more difficult problem of guidance for multiple warheads, with far less space for the guidance system — and far more need for accuracy because of their smaller megatonnage?

In August 1968 there was a widely-publicized test designed to convey the impression to the general public that the MIRVs are ready now. That test was *not* a test of any individually-targeted warheads, which is what the MIRV system is supposed to be. The tests were of Poseidon and Minuteman III rockets. The Poseidon carried only a dummy single warhead. The Minuteman III is alleged to have carried 3 dummy MIRV warheads — but there is no claim that these carried the guidance system which would be necessary for individual targeting.

Furthermore, under present plans, we cannot have *any* Poseidon missiles operational at all until 31 of the Polaris submarines are taken out of service and rebuilt to carry the new and larger Poseidon missiles. Conversion of the Poseidon and Minuteman to MIRVs will *reduce by hundreds* the numbers of ready U.S. missiles during the conversion years.

Anybody who thinks the MIRV is giving us a big jump on the Soviet Union is in for a rude awakening. One week after the U.S. test, the Soviets tested a MIRV which was far bigger and better than ours. Whereas our Minuteman III carried three 500-pound warheads, the Soviet missile carried four 2,500-pound warheads.[5] The Soviets are building MIRVs which are vastly bigger than ours — but they are not foolish enough to substitute MIRVs for their giant weapons capable of destroying America.

chapter IX

WHO ARE TODAY'S ALGER HISSES?

Does the overriding importance of the work of the Rather-Red-than-dead betrayers mean that there is no more Communist infiltration or subversion today? Let's take a brief look at the record.

At the beginning of World War II, the Soviets had planted spies and agents high in the governments of all the Western nations. The Communist espionage network was estimated to consist of 250,000 active agents — 10 times the number employed by all Western governments combined.[1]

Dr. Richard Sorge, who operated in Japan, was probably the master spy of all time. Through his contacts with the Japanese government and especially with another Soviet spy named Ozaki Hozumi, Sorge gave Stalin advance warning of the German attack on Russia in 1941 and of the Japanese attack on the United States at Pearl Harbor.[2] On November 5, 1964 the U.S.S.R. posthumously conferred on Sorge the title "Hero of the Soviet Union."

A retired German officer named Rudolf Roessler set up a clandestine radio station in Lucerne, Switzerland, under the code name "Lucy." With information obtained from ten Soviet agents on the German General Staff, "Lucy" supplied Stalin with the complete details of all German military plans and movements in Russia. This explains why Stalin, with absolutely no military experience, was,

after the initial campaign in 1941, able to antici-
pate all German moves and to earn the title of
Generalissimo of the Soviet armies.[3]

The theft of the atom bomb, called "the crime
of the century," involved Dr. Klaus Fuchs and
Dr. Bruno Pontecorvo in England, Dr. Allan Nunn
May in Canada, and a nest of accomplices in the
United States. Conspiracy is the only explanation
for the meeting one January afternoon in New
York between Klaus Fuchs and Harry Gold, two
men who did not know each other, who did not
use their real names, and who made contact solely
because one man carried a tennis ball, and the
other carried a pair of gloves and a green book.
Fuchs knew all the U.S. atomic secrets and passed
them to Gold.[4] Conspiracy is the only explanation
for the fact that Harry Gold traveled to Albuquer-
que, rang the door of a stranger named David
Greenglass, and presented half of a panel from a
Jello box, found that it matched perfectly with
the other half held by Greenglass, and received
from Greenglass drawings and a written description of the A-bomb trigger mechanism.[5]

The greatest achievement of the Communist
espionage apparatus was the infiltration of the
highest echelons of the U.S. Government.[6] Communist agents included the number-two man in
the State Department, Alger Hiss; the number-
two man in the Treasury Department, Harry Dexter White; a top White House assistant, Lauchlin
Currie; a high official in the Commerce Department, William Remington; a key agent handling
codes in the Government Printing Office, Edward
Rothschild; the Secretary of the International
Monetary Fund, Frank Coe; and a number of
U.S. officials employed by the United Nations.

In the decade following World War II, these and many other Soviet agents were exposed and their stranger-than-fiction adventures made a matter of public record by official investigating bodies in the different countries.[7] However, two additional Soviet spy rings then known to exist in the United States have never been uncovered to this day.[8]

The stars of the Soviet espionage network during the 1950s were Guy Burgess and Donald Maclean, the handsome Englishmen who passed the information to the Soviets, who in turn passed it to the Chinese Reds, that the latter could go ahead and invade Korea without fear of retaliation — because the State Department's secret policy was to tie the hands of General Douglas MacArthur, but give Red China a privileged sanctuary. Thousands of American boys went to their death because of Burgess and Maclean. After they escaped to Moscow, Secretary of the Army Wilbur Brucker said: "Burgess and Maclean had secrets of priceless value to the Communist conspiracy."[9]

Other top Soviet spies during the late 1950s were Bernon Mitchell and William Martin, cipher experts in the National Security Agency who stole U.S. codes and secret messages and then fled to Moscow via Havana.[10]

Evidence is already unfolding about the Communist spies and agents of the 1960s. The largest number of important Soviet spies has been uncovered in England.[11] Soviet spies operating there who passed top military and technical secrets to Moscow included Kim Philby, William Vassall, George Blake, Gordon Lonsdale, Harry Houghton, Ethel Gee, Peter and Helen Kroger. The Lonsdale spy ring concentrated on stealing the secrets of nuclear submarines and anti-submarine warfare. Philby brags in his recent memoirs published in Moscow that he had a permanent unrestricted pass to the Atomic Energy Commission building in Washington, D.C. Soviet penetration of Britain is so complete that one important convicted spy, George Blake, was spirited out of a heavily-guarded British prison and taken to Moscow to receive his reward.

Israel found that one of its most trusted citizens, Dr. Israel Beer, was a longtime Soviet agent who transmitted war plans to Moscow during the 1956 war with Egypt.[12] His defection caused Ben Gurion to exclaim, "I am surrounded by treachery!"

Philippe Thyraud de Vosjoli, a French intelligence chief, defected to the United States in 1968 because he believes that "General de Gaulle's government is so riddled with Soviet spies that it represents a grave threat to Western civilization."[13]

Sweden was shocked to discover that one of its most prominent and trusted diplomats stationed in Washington, D.C., Stig Wennerstroem, had been sending Swedish, U.S., and NATO secrets to the Soviets for 15 years. At the same time that he was a Colonel in the Swedish Air Force, he was secretly drawing a salary as a Major General in the Soviet Army.[14]

Brazil discovered in the nick of time in 1964 that its president was a militant pro-Communist, and perhaps a secret Communist, and that he had put 28 Communists into key administrative posts in the Brazilian government.[15]

The government of Bolivia was shaken in July 1968 when it became known that the Minister of the Interior was a secret ally of Fidel Castro and smuggled to him the diary of Che Guevara describing Che's efforts to capture South America by guerrilla warfare from bases in the Andes.[16]

What About The U.S.?

Are we to assume that the Soviets, having successfully penetrated the highest levels of our Government in the 1940s and 1950s, and having successfully continued their penetration of the governments of nearly all other Western nations through the 1960s, have terminated their espionage in America? To believe this would be the height of ostrich-like self-deception. A realistic assessment requires us to assume that the Soviets have not only continued, but accelerated, their penetration in the United States.

The historical record of Communist infiltration is ample evidence for all those who are not blinded by liberal prejudices, but it is well to note the corroborative warning given us by Colonel Oleg Penkovskiy. A senior officer in Soviet military intelligence who defected to the West and gave us much valuable information, he graphically described the omnipresence of the Soviet network:

"We spy everywhere.[17] . . . Espionage is conducted by the Soviet government on such a gigantic scale that an outsider has difficulty in fully comprehending it. To be naive and to underestimate it is a grave mistake.[18] . . .

"Everything is being stolen right from under their noses, and they are doing nothing to fight the Communists.[19] . . . The West builds or conducts costly scientific research work in some scientific or technical field while the Soviets just sit and wait and collect information on this work.[20] . . ."

One of the documents which Penkovskiy leaked out of the Kremlin is the verbatim transcript of a lecture given to the GRU by Colonel Dzikhodko. It is a fascinating document giving in great detail a Soviet espionage agent's view of the United States and the American people. It shows how Soviet agents can circle around our strengths and play on our weaknesses in order to secure the information they want and to entrap enough U.S. citizens to help them do so.[21]

Current proof of the penetration of the U.S. Government was given by Colonel Michal Goleniewski of the Polish Army military intelligence. From April 1958 to December 1960, he transmitted to the United States via Henry J. Taylor, U.S. Minister to Switzerland, 160 pages of typewritten reports and some 5,000 pages of microfilmed documents on Soviet intelligence. On January 12, 1961, Goleniewski was flown in an Air Force transport to Washington, D.C. where he signed contract B-39752 with the CIA to brief U.S. authorities in regard to Soviet agents. A grateful Congress enacted H.R. 5507, a special bill which bestowed American citizenship and said that Goleniewski had rendered "major contributions to the national security of the United States."

The list of Soviet agents exposed by Goleniewski included such important spies as Colonel Stig Wennerstroem, who had access to an American strategic air base where many U.S. Air Force personnel were not allowed; Gordon Lonsdale, who headed the British spy ring which stole our Polaris submarine secrets; George Blake, the British intelligence officer who was a secret KGB agent; and Dr. Israel Beer who told the Soviets of Israel's 1956 Suez war plans.

Goleniewski, a former Iron Curtain intelligence officer, told his U.S. interrogators there were persons high in the U.S. Government known to him as agents of the Soviet KGB. He said that at least three American scientists with access to defense secrets were on the KGB payroll for services constantly rendered. He told of a number of KGB agents in the State Department: three at the embassy counselor level, two in the security branch, and several others in the code and communications sections. He referred to several in the CIA. Goleniewski said that the KGB has infiltrated American embassies in cities abroad and every important U. S. agency "except the FBI."[22]

There is no basis for the JFK-LBJ-HHH assumption that Soviet espionage and influence inside our government ceased when they took office. Why can't the Alger Hisses and Harry Dexter Whites and Owen Lattimores of the 1960s be exposed and rooted out of government? There are two reasons.

Rostow vs. Otepka

The first reason is that the JFK-LBJ-HHH Administrations for 8 years have deliberately prevented any investigation of Communists in Government and have suspended nearly all security precautions to keep them out. This is what the famous Otto Otepka case is all about.[23]

After the Kennedy-Johnson Administration was elected in 1960, one of its first acts was to try to appoint Dr. Walt W. Rostow to a high post in the State Department. Dean Rusk and Bobby Kennedy confronted the State Department's chief security officer, Otto Otepka, with a demand that Rostow be approved. Otepka refused to relax the security requirements for Rostow who had been three times rejected for employment by the Eisenhower Administration for security reasons.

Bobby Kennedy then staged a tantrum, referring to the U.S. Air Force as "a bunch of jerks;" but he knew that Otepka had the law on his side. So Rostow was appointed to a position inside the White House where there appear to be no security restrictions at all. Rostow's position in the LBJ Administration is called "Special Assistant to the President for National Security Affairs." He is, in fact, the principal foreign policy adviser of the Johnson Administration. It was Rostow who awakened the President at one o'clock in the morning to inform him of the capture of the Pueblo.

When Harlan Cleveland was named Assistant Secretary of State in 1961, Otepka's office found him not qualified even for a temporary security clearance. Thereupon, Dean Rusk simply waived the security requirement and appointed Cleveland anyway.

In July 1962, Cleveland asked Otepka "if there were any prospects for the reemployment of Alger Hiss in the United States Government." Otepka pointed out that Hiss had been convicted of a felony and therefore is ineligible for Federal employment. The felony, of course, was perjury for denying that he had given secret Government documents to Soviet agents.

In August 1962, Cleveland set up an Advisory Committee on International Organizations. He personally appointed the members and informed Otepka that he was avoiding a security investigation by invoking "waiver" procedures. At least one of these men had served on the personal staff of Alger Hiss in the State Department and three had close and intimate associations with him and stated that they did not believe Hiss was guilty.

On September 9, 1965, LBJ promoted Cleveland to serve as U.S. Ambassador to NATO.

By 1962, Otepka became aware that Rusk had granted 152 security "waivers" to high State Department officials. This figure compares with only two such waivers granted during 8 years of the Eisenhower Administration. Otepka listed and described 18 security risks holding important positions in the State Department.

The result of Otepka's efforts was that the security risks were retained and promoted, while Otepka became the victim of the most unrelenting campaign of harassment and intimidation in the history of the U.S. Civil Service. His telephone was tapped, his safe rifled, and his wastebaskets searched. He was put under surveillance, locked out of his office, placed in isolation, reduced in grade, barred from security duties, and finally put on leave without pay.

Senators who have studied the case say that Otto Otepka is the best-qualified man in Government to carry out the housecleaning in the State Department which our country has needed for 30 years. Nothing but a change of Administration can ever give him the chance.

"The Garbage Pail Of Our History"

The second reason why the Alger Hisses of the 1960s cannot be exposed and turned out of Government office is that the Supreme Court has voided most of our legal safeguards against Communism.

When in November 1965 the Supreme Court knocked out the 1950 Internal Security Act requirement that individual Communists must register, U.S. Communist Party boss Gus Hall boasted that another anti-Communist law had been tossed into "the garbage pail of our national history."[24]

Hall had a right to boast. Here is a brief summary of the legal safeguards against Communism which the Supreme Court has tossed into "the garbage pail of our national history."

1) It knocked out the anti-subversion laws of the 50 states (*Pennsylvania v. Steve Mesarosh*).

2) It voided the convictions of many leading Communists because, said the Court, they were only engaged in advocacy of Communism, not action (*Yates et al v. U.S.*).

3) It put unnecessary restrictions on the FBI (*Jencks v. U.S.*).

4) It struck down the Internal Security law forbidding passports to Communists (*Aptheker. v. Secretary of State*). When Stokely Carmichael returned from an illegal trip in 1967 to Cuba and North Vietnam where he attacked the United States and U.S. troops, the State Department picked up his passport. In the summer of 1968, the State Department quietly returned Carmichael's passport, saying that Supreme Court decisions required this.

5) It nullified the Subversive Activities Control Act by ruling that the Communist Party did not have to register (*Albertson v. Subversive Activities Control Board*).

6) It ruled that it was a violation of the "right of association" for Congress to forbid the employment of known Communists in defense jobs (*U.S. v. Robel*).

7) It struck down the section of the Taft-Hartley Law which forbade Communists from serving as union officers (*U.S. v. Archie Brown —*

Brown will be remembered as the chief agitator in the documentary film *Operation Abolition).*

8) It ruled unconstitutional many state Loyalty Oath programs *(Baggett v. Bullitt* and *Whitehill v. Elkins).*

9) It weakened the Industrial Security Program by ordering the Navy to give top security clearance to an engineer whose sister-in-law, a nuclear physicist, entertained Soviet spies in his home and then defected to Red China to help it develop atomic and hydrogen bombs *(Greene v. Secretary of Defense).*

10) It so restricted the activities of the State and Congressional Committees charged with investigating Communism that they can no longer effectively investigate espionage inside the U.S. *(Watkins v. U.S., Yellin v. U.S., Russell v. U.S., Dombrowski v. Pfister, Gibson v. Florida Legislative Investigation Committee).*

11) It awarded back pay to numerous persons discharged by the Federal Government as security risks *(Service v. Dulles, Greene v. U.S., Cole v. Young, Vitarelli v. Secretary of Interior).*

The Decency Gap

Although the Supreme Court has been tossing anti-Communist legislation into "the garbage pail of our national history" since Red Monday of 1957, the majority had in general held the line against hard-core pornography by five-to-four decisions. When President Johnson appointed his friend, Abe Fortas, to the Court, this tipped the scales in favor of pornography and started a series of decisions which caused Congress in Public Law 90-100 to declare that "the traffic in obscenity and pornography is a matter of national concern."

Fortas' efforts to change U.S. opposition to pornography began before he became a Supreme Court Justice. In 1955, lawyer Fortas was paid $11,000 by William Hamling to obtain a second-class mailing permit for his indecent magazine, *Rogue*. Up until that time, magazines trafficking in pornography

had been unable to obtain second-class mailing permits which are extremely valuable because they mean great savings in postage. By statute, second-class permits are supposed to be issued only for reading material "published for the dissemination of information of a public character, or devoted to literature, to science, arts, or a special industry."[25]

Testimony before the Senate Judiciary Committee revealed that an FBI agent named Homer Young had been told by Hamling that he had hired Abe Fortas as a lawyer because Fortas "could fix anything no matter what administration was in power."

After Fortas succeeded in obtaining second-class mail permits for *Rogue* and *Playboy*, the Postmaster General felt obliged to issue similar second-class permits to other indecent magazines. In 1960, a Federal Court ordered the Postmaster General to issue second-class permits to two nudist magazines which illustrate, "advocate and explain nudism and the nudist mode of living" because, said the Court, similar permits have been issued to *Rogue*, *Playboy*,   *Dude*,   etc.[26]

In 1957 lawyer Fortas filed a brief for Hamling's Greenleaf Publishing Company, the then publisher of *Rogue*, and argued that the conviction of a pornographer named Roth should be set aside because Federal statues against obscenity were "unconstitutional."[27]

After Fortas was appointed to the Supreme Court, he voted on June 12, 1967 to reverse a conviction by the Georgia courts that a paperback named *Sin Whisper*, published by Corinth Publications (another company owned by William Hamling), was obscene. Before handing down this decision, Justice Fortas and the majority did not even give the State of Georgia a chance to file a brief or present arguments in support of the Georgia court decisions.

Justice Fortas did not excuse himself when the Supreme Court heard this case involving his former client, William Hamling.[28]

Fortas cast the deciding vote to reverse the conviction by the California courts of an exhibitor, in an arcade frequented by youths, of three nudie peep show films entitled "0.7", "0.12" and "D-15".[29] In holding these films obscene, Federal District Judge Hauk had said:

> "The appeal of the films, taken as a whole, is to a shameful and morbid interest in nudity, sex, and the female organs of sex and excretion. . . . The court concludes as a matter of law that the exhibits and each of them are clearly, unequivocally and incontrovertibly obscene and pornographic in the hard-core sense. . . ."[30]

During 1967 and 1968, Justice Fortas voted to reverse 40 convictions for publication of obscene movies, books and magazines. There were only two cases in which lower-court convictions for obscenity were affirmed by the Supreme Court, plus one holding a conviction moot, and in all three cases Fortas voted to reverse the convictions and let the guilty go free.[31] In *Jacobs v. New York*, Fortas was the only Justice who voted to overturn the conviction of the exhibitor of the obscene film

Flaming Creatures, an underground movie involving nudity, rapes, and acts of male and female perversion.

Representatives of the Citizens for Decent Literature told the Senate Judiciary Committee in August 1968:

> "As a result of these decisions, the market is now flooded with material that previously had been available only in the Black Market . . . a new class of girlie magazines featuring still photos taken from stag movies . . . so-called nudist magazines which feature exposure of the pubic and rectal areas . . . the new class of paperback books with very innocuous covers . . . but containing hard-core pornography within."

When the Communists came to power in Soviet Russia, they sneered at morality and family life as "bourgeois" relics from the capitalist system which should be eliminated. Free love was to be a part of the new Red order. In a few years they reaped a harvest of juvenile delinquency, crime, and a plummeting birth rate. In desperation, the Reds restored the family and backed it with a strict code of morality which swiftly punished any suggestion of indecency in print, picture, stage or screen. The new policy paid off and Soviet Russia became strong, producing vigorous, disciplined young men and women who scored impressive triumphs in the Olympics and make good soldiers.

At the same time, the Communists began promoting immorality in the United States because of its destructive effect on our national fiber. Their success has taken a sharp upward turn since 1965.

chapter X

THE SOLUTION

Lyndon Johnson's once-favorite story, told by him often to personal friends, but always in confidence, was leaked to the public only through the spite of some reporters whom he had offended. He called it his "Luci's Little Monks Story." Parts of the story have been reported in the press,[1] but the information it revealed on what has happened to the strategic strength of America in the LBJ Administration has not been reported elsewhere. Here is the story:

It was a rainy night in Washington on June 28, 1966, and Luci, not yet married, came home to the White House about 10 P.M. She found her father pacing the room with a deeply troubled expression on his face. She asked if she could help. Sit down and learn some history, her father replied,

"Your daddy may go down in history as having started World War III.

"You may not wake up tomorrow."

President Johnson then explained to Luci that he had finally brought himself to the decision that the U.S. must attack the oil-storage facilities at Haiphong, North Vietnam, and had ordered U.S. bombers to make the strike. He said he had asked for picked crews on our aircraft, and the pilots were ordered not to release their bombs unless they could see the targets because he was worried that they might bomb the wrong target

— perhaps a Soviet ship. Yet, despite all the precautions he had ordered, he was still worried that something might go wrong. A miscalculation could mean that Washington, and the whole world could be turned into a holocaust.

Luci replied that, when she had worries, she went to what she called her "Little Monks" at St. Dominic's Catholic Church in southwest Washington, and prayed. She suggested that, although it was late, they do the same. Lyndon Johnson, recalling that a business partner once told him that, in times of trouble, heavy thinking and deep praying were a comfort, agreed.

So, together with Mrs. Johnson and Patrick Nugent, Luci's husband-to-be, they drove through the rain to St. Dominic's and knelt in silent prayer. After their return to the White House, the reports of the bombing raid came in. There had been no miscalculation; no Soviet ship had been hit.

The President told the story to personal friends many times during the following year. When he told it at a White House party for Supreme Court Justices on May 11, 1967, it made its way into the press for the first time.

The "Luci's Little Monks Story" revealed far, far more than LBJ's love for Luci. When he expressed the fear that a little bombing raid in Vietnam might cause the Soviets to attack America with nuclear weapons, and that Luci might not wake up in the morning because Washington might be destroyed in a nuclear holocaust during the night, President Johnson proved:

1) that we do not have the nuclear strength to deter a Soviet attack on the U.S.;

2) that we have no defense to protect ourselves from destruction if they do attack; and

3) that the loss of our nuclear strength ties our hands from effective action everywhere in the world, even in defense of our servicemen and our own vital interests.

Political action *now* is the best solution to the problems facing our nation. If a football manager had 8 years of consecutive defeats, after being given the most money and talent, the fans would all agree that it's time for a change and suspect that some games were being "thrown." If the evidence showed the defeats were planned, they would *throw* the manager out.

There are those who say that the infiltration of Government and deterioration of morals are so extensive that there is no hope without a restoration of spiritual values and a return to God.

We must not confuse personal salvation with national survival. These are two different objectives which call for two different solutions.

The people of Poland are as religious as any nation on earth. Nearly all will undoubtedly achieve personal salvation. But their genuine religious fervor did not save their country from national disaster. They were betrayed at the top by Stalin, Churchill, and Franklin Roosevelt. "Betrayed" was precisely the word used by our own U.S. Ambassador, Arthur Bliss Lane, who told how it was done in his book *I Saw Poland Betrayed.*

The people of Hungary are a good and courageous people. They have been fighting the battles of Christianity and holding the gates of Europe against the Asiatic invaders for 2,000 years. But when the Soviet troops and tanks rolled into Budapest, the whole world could describe the result in only one word — "butchery."

The people of China are a moral people. They were not afflicted with any of the problems our country has today. They had no juvenile delinquency, no pornography, no students shouting obscene words, no hippies, no draft-card burners, no rising crime. But morality did not save them. They were betrayed by Owen Lattimore and the pro-Communist China crowd in the State Department.[2] Because of that betrayal, 600,000,000 Chinese were taken over by the Communists, there were 157,000 American casualties in the Korean War, there are already 200,000 casualties in the Vietnam War, and the end is not yet.

In nearly all the captive nations, the religion and morality of the people had virtually no effect on the fate of their nation because that fate was decided in Moscow and Washington.

It is essential to work for personal salvation, for a return to religion, and for a restoration of the moral fiber of our people. But this will not save America from criminals or Communists. There is no evidence that a robber or rapist cares whether his victim is virtuous or not. Prayer is necessary, but should not be used as an excuse for *not* doing the hard and courageous things which must be done if our nation is to survive. The best formula is: Pray as if it were all up to God, and work as if it were all up to us.

What We Can Do

Here are the fundamental objectives most Americans yearn for:

1. To restore law and order to our cities.
2. To win without more delay the "no-win"

war in Vietnam, and to end the policies which bring on more Vietnams.

3. To protect our homes from a nuclear attack and from suicidal nuclear disarmament.

4. To clean up the rampant corruption in Washington and end the coddling of security risks and influence peddlers.

5. To restore fiscal sanity and local self-government.

There probably are several roads which will ultimately lead to the attainment of these objectives, but absolutely nothing can give us as big a leap toward them as a complete housecleaning in the Federal Government in November 1968. It is the *only* thing we know we *can* accomplish this year. It is the best and most practical single step we can take toward restoring sanity to our nation and assuring its survival.

We are fortunate that there is a general national election in November 1968. Nothing should take precedence over the immediate and pressing task of sweeping out of office all those who have betrayed our nation by exposing us to the attacks of criminals and Communists. There is nothing wrong with America that cannot be cured by a complete clean-out from Washington of those who brought our country to its perilous condition.

The first part of this housecleaning task is the election of Senators and Congressmen, as well as state and local officials, who stand *for* law and order and *against* the Kerner Report and the phony poverty program; who stand *for* restoring U.S. nuclear superiority and *against* the McNamara-Nitze policies; who stand *for* victory in Vietnam and *against* a "camouflaged surrender"; who stand *for* the removal of security risks and *against* trade with Communist countries; who stand *for* sound money and *against* deficits.

Ask your candidates where they stand. Make them commit themselves publicly *before* the election. After the election, keep track of them and hold them to their promises. There are some splendid patriots in Congress today, but not nearly enough. We need about a hundred more with backbone if we are to have a real change.

If you are in doubt as to whether to support a Republican or Democratic Congressman, and if you are tired of high taxes and of inflation caused by Federal deficits, then consider the comparative record of the two Parties on fiscal policy. In this century, 1900 through 1968, Republicans held the White House for 33 years and the Democrats 36 years. Here is the record.

Republicans increased your personal taxes only once, the Democrats increased your taxes 13 times. Republicans reduced your taxes six times, Democrats reduced them four times. Republicans balanced the Federal budget 21 years out of 33, the Democrats balanced the budget six years out of 36. Republicans had deficits 12 years out of 33 years, the Democrats had deficits 30 out of 36 years. The cumulative deficits under Republicans amount to $22 billion, under the Democrats $314 billion.

What About The Presidency?

Many good Americans, demanding perfection and dissatisfied with the three alternatives, have decided to forget about the Presidency and work only for Congressional races. Such a decision is out of touch with all political reality because the power of the Executive has so far outstripped the power of Congress.

Congress has 25,000 employees and the Executive has 3,000,000 — and that is just about the ratio of their respective power in Washington today. In addition, the Executive has the spending power (which, under the present Administration, has been used ruthlessly to whip Congressmen into line), the power of appointments, and the power of foreign policy which may be decisive as to the future of our country. A responsible citizen today cannot default on his decision and say it doesn't matter who is elected President.

In the field of defense, Congress tried valiantly in 1966 and 1967 to bring about a change in the disastrous McNamara policies. The House Armed Services Committee issued a Report, signed by all Democratic and Republican members, which was an across-the-board indictment of the McNamara policies. Then Congress, in a near-unanimous vote, appropriated money for certain pre-production engineering on the Nike X antimissile. But the power of the Executive was so great that McNamara and Nitze successfully defied Congress and refused to spend the money for the weapon Congress ordered.

Whom should we support for President?

Hubert Humphrey stands, of course, for a continuation of all the disastrous policies of the Johnson Administration. The election of Humphrey would mean that the McNamara, Nitze, and Ramsey Clark policies would remain intact, even if the Cabinet officers are changed.

It is rather well-known in Washington that Humphrey plans to name as Secretary of State George Wildman Ball, who would be even worse than Dean Rusk. Ball is the author of the secret Ball Report which was the master plan for the foreign economic policy of the Johnson Administration. The thesis of the Ball Report was that we must "seek an accommodation with the Soviet Union." It advocated a vast increase of U.S. credit to and trade with Communist countries even in strategic items, and the repeal of the Battle Act and other laws prohibiting strategic war goods and credits to the Communist bloc.[3] It was Ball who persuaded LBJ to remove on October 7, 1966 more than 400 strategic items, including our latest model computers and machine tools for making weapons, from the list of goods forbidden to be shipped to Iron Curtain countries.

Ball is one of the principal gravediggers in our Government today. That he has long been singled out by the Establishment for high office is indicated by his attendance at the secret meeting of the Bilderbergers in 1957 at St. Simon's Island.[4] George Ball has frankly stated that, if he becomes Secretary of State, Otto Otepka will never be permitted to set foot inside the State Department.

The election of Hubert Humphrey would be a continuation of the present policies of appeasement, payment of blackmail, and eventual surrender to Communists and criminals. These policies have caused the decline of the American Republic. They will cause its fall if continued for four more years.

What about George Wallace? Many good people are casting a hopeful eye on this man who comes riding the third-party horse, promising to change our disastrous foreign policies. He says: "There is not ten cents worth of difference between the two major political parties. The American Independent Party is the only hope for a real change."

History shows that a third party, however well-intentioned and well-financed, and however able and articulate its leader and dedicated its workers, cannot succeed in its first venture. General John C. Fremont, the handsome, glamorous first candidate of the Republican Party, could capture only 33% of the popular vote in 1856. Theodore Roosevelt, running as a very popular ex-President, with all the contacts and support which his magnetic personality commanded, could not defeat the two-party system. Senator Robert LaFollette, the dynamic Progressive Party candidate for President in 1924, received only 16% of the popular vote, although his platform was very similar to the New Deal program so successful in 1932, 1936 and 1940.

George Wallace is fond of saying that there isn't any real difference between Nixon and Humphrey — both of them are just Vice Presidents. Nixon's rejoinder is: "Yes, but Mr. Humphrey and I trained under different Presidents."

There is real substance behind this quip. The difference between Nixon and Humphrey is *at least* as much as the difference between Eisenhower and Lyndon Johnson. Let us examine what that difference is.

The War and Peace Gap

No one can deny that the Eisenhower Administration failed to clean out the State Department, and was wrong on Castro, Nasser, Hungary, and Earl Warren. But let us not forget the plus side of the ledger. During the Eisenhower Administration, we established and maintained peace through strength — and no new foreign wars were allowed to bring any American boys to their deaths. On the other hand, four of the last five Democrat Presidents have led us into four bloody foreign wars. None of the last six Republican Presidents has involved us in any war.

In 1916, Woodrow Wilson won reelection on the slogan "He kept us out of war." Within a few months, he had the United States involved in World War I.

In 1940, Franklin Roosevelt won reelection with this famous promise: "Mothers and fathers, I give you one more assurance. I have said this before, but I shall say it again and again and again. Your boys are not going to be sent into any foreign wars." This line was put into Roosevelt's speech by ghost-writer Robert Sherwood, and today even the Roosevelt lovers no longer try to defend it. The historical fact is that Roosevelt, in the words of his own Secretary of War, Henry Stimson, tried to "maneuver them [the Japanese] into the position of firing the first shot without allowing too much danger to ourselves."

On June 1, 1950, Harry Truman said: "We are closer to peace now than at any time in the last five years." Within a month, he had us involved in the Korean War.

In 1964, the Democrats sponsored those infamous television spots which showed a little girl picking daisies being incinerated in an atomic mushroom cloud. These spots were deliberately designed to mislead the voters into believing that Barry Goldwater was a trigger-happy warmonger. We now know that, at the same time in 1964 that Lyndon Johnson was promising peace, he was committing American boys to fight the same type of a land war in Asia, with privileged sanctuaries for the enemy, which had cost us so many lives in Korea.

America is never so close to war as when the Democrats are promising peace. The American voters have been deceived again and again and again. By now the voters should know that the surest key to peace is to elect a Republican President.

Johnson and Humphrey plead that they seek peace. But as long as it is a "peace" based on the McNamara-Nitze policies, the word which should be used is "surrender." It is the "peace" of Prague, the "peace" of Budapest, the "peace" of Havana. That is not the kind of peace Americans want or deserve. But if we don't clean house in 1968, it is the only kind of peace we have a chance of having.

Likewise, on the great issue of an adequate defense, the difference between the Eisenhower-Nixon Administration and the Johnson-Humphrey Administration is the difference between defense and disarmament. In the election of 1968, this means that your vote can be a vote for survival — or it can be a vote for surrender to nuclear blackmail or attack.

Weapons may be complicated — and in the nuclear age they certainly are — but the principles of war and peace remain the same. Weakness invites attack from greedy aggressors. Military strength is our basic guarantee of continued freedom and independence. Every nuclear weapon defending America today was built or ordered under the Eisenhower Administration, including the Minuteman and Titan missiles, the Polaris submarines, and the B-52 and B-58 bombers.

The Republican position — so successful under

President Eisenhower, and still valid now — is based on a posture of overwhelming military superiority over any possible aggressors. This is the only policy which will keep us out of war and safe from nuclear attack. We have lost eight years' time. We haven't another year to lose. This is the urgent message given us by all military experts who have spoken out on this subject. This is why General Curtis LeMay entitled his 1968 book *America Is In Danger*.

Our military experts, like the FBI, can only give us the facts. They cannot enforce the policies they recommend. Only the politicians can do that — and only the voters have control over the politicians. That is why the problem today calls for political action as the prime solution.

Does this mean that Richard Nixon is the answer to all our problems and will change our country overnight? Of course not. In his acceptance speech in Miami, Nixon said, "I do not promise the millenium in the morning." He knows no candidate can do that. But he did promise in his acceptance speech in Miami:

"We shall restore the strength of America — so that we shall always negotiate from strength and never from weakness."

The change necessary to save America from being either Red or dead requires the work, the contribution, and the vote of every American. Our nation cannot survive four more years of betrayal.

REFERENCES

I. Not Sick — But Betrayed

1. *U.S. News & World Report,* Sept. 9, 1968, p. 12.
2. *UPI Dispatch,* Aug. 29, 1968.
3. June 17, 1858.
4. After his reelection in 1936, President Franklin Roosevelt won a reversal of the Supreme Court attitude toward New Deal legislation before he made a single appointment to the Court.

II. Why Do They Betray Us?

1. *Chicago Tribune,* Sept. 5, 6, and 7, 1968.

III. Why the Soviets Invaded Czechoslovakia

1. *Time,* Aug. 30, 1968, p. 22; *Newsweek,* Sept. 2, 1968, p. 14.
2. *Washington Post* Dispatch, Prague, Aug. 29, 1968; confirmed by UPI Dispatch, Prague, Aug. 31, 1968.
3. Reuters Dispatch, Aug. 31, 1968.
4. *The New York Times,* Sept. 1, 1968.
5. Harry Hopkins.
6. For example, see Senators William Fulbright and Joseph Clark, *The Elite and the Electorate,* 1963.
7. Agreement negotiated between Czech and Soviet leaders at Cierna, July 29, 1968; embodied in Joint Declaration of "unity" of Communist nations by Warsaw Pact Leaders, Aug. 3, 1968; as a result, Soviet troops were withdrawn from Czechoslovakia — obviously in preparation for the surprise attack.
8. UPI Dispatch, Geneva, Aug. 29, 1968. *Time,* Aug. 30, 1968, p. 14. *St. Louis Post-Dispatch,* Sept. 1, 1968.
9. Aug. 27, 1968.
10. *St. Louis Post-Dispatch,* Sept. 10, 1962.
11. *Washington Post* Dispatch, Prague, Sept. 1, 1968.
12. Speech to the Commonwealth Club, reported in *The Commonwealth,* Aug. 12, 1968.
13. *Manchester Guardian* Dispatch, Sept. 4, 1968.
14. Column, Sept. 3, 1968.

IV. Planned Defeat

1. Speech to the American Society of Newspaper Editors, Apr. 20, 1961.
2. The facts and quotations in this chapter are from the U.S. Senate Internal Security Subcommittee Report on *Communist Threat to the United States Through the Caribbean,* Part 13.
3. *The Saturday Evening Post,* May 21, 1966, p. 31.

V. Victory Betrayed

1. Mario Lazo, "The Cuban Missile Crisis: Who Won?", *Reader's Digest*, Sept. 1968, p. 130, 138.
2. Syndicated Column, Oct. 13, 1962.
3. Philippe Thyraud de Vosjoli, "The Strange Case of de Gaulle and the Soviet Spies," *Reader's Digest*, July 1968, p. 95, 98.
4. Quoted in Walter Lippmann Column, Oct. 13, 1962.
5. Roger Hilsman, *To Move A Nation*, 1967, p. 195.
6. James Daniel and John G. Hubbell, *Strike in the West*, 1963.
7. Los Angeles Times, Dec. 15, 1962.
8. Mario Lazo, *Dagger in the Heart: American Policy Failures in Cuba*, 1968.

VI. The Nitze Surrender Plan

1. *The Communist Manifesto*.
2. *U.S. News & World Report*, Dec. 27, 1957, p. 32.
3. *The New York Times*, Aug. 3, 1967.
4. Donald Seaman & John Mather, *The Great Spy Scandal*, 1955, p. 56; Page, Leitch & Knightley, *The Philby Conspiracy*, 1968, p. 226.
5. A fuller description of Nitze's Asilomar speech is given in Schlafly & Ward, *The Gravediggers*, Chapter 6. A description of Nitze's Report on nuclear strategy for the National Council of Churches is given in Schlafly & Ward, *Strike from Space*, Chapter 13.
6. In addition to the evidence presented in this chapter, see the following sources: Gen. Curtis E. LeMay and Maj. Gen. Dale O. Smith, *America Is In Danger*. Gen. Nathan Twining, *Neither Liberty Nor Safety*. William Kintner, *Peace and the Strategy Conflict*. U.S. News & World Report, Feb. 6, 1967, p. 34-37; Feb. 20, 1967, p. 84-86; July 24, 1967, p. 32-34; Feb. 26, 1968, p. 84-86; Mar. 18, 1968, p. 82; May 6, 1968, p. 14; July 15, 1968, p. 28. *Washington Reports* of the American Security Council, especially Sept. 18, 1967. Congressman Melvin R. Laird, "The Need for a Blue Ribbon Commission," *Congressional Record*, June 28, 1966. Congressman Craig Hosmer, "Megatons Do Count," July 23, 1967. Hanson W. Baldwin, "Threats and Counter-threats," *The New York Times Book Review*, Oct. 22, 1967. "The Myth of Technological Stalemate," *Air Force and Space Digest*, Mar., 1967. "Balance of Terror," *Barron's*, Feb. 5, 1968. "The Threat of Russia's Rising Strategic Power," *Reader's Digest*, Feb. 1968.
7. This is now admitted by all the liberal press; e.g., St. Louis Post-Dispatch, June 2, 1968.
8. Roy Neal, *Ace in the Hole: The Story of the Minuteman*, p. 168.

9. *Newsweek*, Jan. 12, 1965.
10. U.S. Senate Foreign Relations Committee Hearings, Aug. 13, 1963, p. 100.
11. *The Saturday Evening Post*, June 20, 1964, p. 15.
12. AP Dispatch, Aug. 28, 1968.
13. *The New York Times*, July 5, 1968.
14. AP Dispatch, July 5, 1968.
15. For additional information, see *Research and Development: Our Neglected Weapon*, published by the Republican National Committee, May 1968, and prepared by former Secretary of Defense Neil H. McElroy, former Secretary of Defense Thomas S. Gates, Jr., et al.
16. Gen. Thomas S. Power, *Design for Survival*, p. 161. An attractive new illustrated adaptation of this fine book for mass readership is available from American Security Council, 123 N. Wacker Dr., Chicago, Ill., 25¢. See also, Roy Neal, *Ace in the Hole*, p. 168.
17. *U.S. News & World Report*, July 15, 1968, p. 28.
18. Hearings on the Nuclear Test Ban Treaty, Aug. 15, 1963, pp. 273-274.
19. A fuller account of the TFX story is given in Schlafly, *Safe—Not Sorry*, Chapters 6 & 7.
20. *U.S. News & World Report*, Apr. 8, 1968, p. 16.
21. *Standard Oil Co. of California v. Moore*, 251 F. 2d 188, 210.

VII. The Living Lie

1. Pittsburgh, Pa., Oct. 19, 1932.
2. Radio address at Albany, N.Y., July 30, 1932.
3. Sioux City, Ia., Sept. 29, 1932.
4. Oleg Penkovskiy, *The Penkovskiy Papers*, 1965, p. 55.
5. Ibid., p. 203.
6. Dean Acheson, "McNamara: Technocrat or Statesman?", *Book World*, Aug. 25, 1968.
7. Gen. Albert C. Wedemeyer, *Wedemeyer Reports*, 1958, p. 376. See also, Dr. Anthony Kubek, *How The Far East Was Lost*, 1963, pp. 317-343.
8. Robert S. McNamara, *The Essence of Security: Reflections in Office*, 1968, p. x.
9. Congressman Craig Hosmer, Statement of Nov. 6, 1967.
10. *The Essence of Security*, p. 52.
11. AP Dispatch, Aug. 15, 1968.
12. *Time*, Aug. 11, 1967. Also confirmed by AP Dispatch, July 29, 1967. Air Force Secretary Harold Brown substantially conceded the accuracy of the reports.
13. *The Essence of Security*, p. 55.
14. U.S. Senate Foreign Relations Committee, Hearings on the Nuclear Test Ban Treaty, Aug. 13, 1963, p. 100.

15. Ibid., Aug. 15, 1963, pp. 273-274.
16. *The Essence of Security*, p. 56.
17. Ibid., p. 63.
18. For a fuller explanation of the Nike X anti-missile, see Schlafly & Ward, *Strike From Space*, Chapter 21.
19. *The Essence of Security*, p. 64.
20. Center for Strategic Studies, *The Soviet Military Technological Challenge*, 1967, p. xii.
21. *The Essence of Security*, p. 76.
22. See Schlafly & Ward, *Strike From Space*, p. 225.
23. *The Essence of Security*, p. 81.
24. *Washington Post* Dispatch, Aug. 29, 1968.
25. *The Essence of Security*, p. 67.
26. Ibid., p. 109.

VIII. The Myth of the MIRVs

1. House Report 1536, May 16, 1966.
2. See fuller explanation in Schlafly & Ward, *Strike from Space*, pp. 109-112.
3. Summary of the evidence prepared by William L. Borden, executive director of the Congressional Joint Committee on Atomic Energy.
4. "A Russian Scientist's Blueprint for Mankind," translated from the Russian by *The New York Times*, July 25, 1968.
5. *Newsweek*, Sept. 9, 1968, p. 19.

IX. Who Are Today's Alger Hisses?

1. E. H. Cookridge, *The Net That Covers the World*, 1955. U.S. Committee on Un-American Activities, *Patterns of Communist Espionage*, 1959. By 1960, the figure had climbed to 300,000, according to an official report of the U.S. State Department, published in *U.S. News & World Report*, June 27, 1960, p. 70.
2. Maj. Gen. Charles A. Willoughby, *Shanghai Conspiracy*, 1952.
3. Pierre Accoce and Pierre Quet, *A Man Called Lucy*, 1966.
4. U.S. House Committee on Un-American Activities, *Chronicle of Treason*, 1958.
5. Ralph de Toledano, *The Greatest Plot in History*, 1963, pp. 207-209.
6. U.S. Senate Internal Security Subcommittee, *Interlocking Subversion in Government Departments*, 1953. Robert E. Stripling, *The Red Plot Against America*, 1949. James Burnham, *The Web of Subversion*, 1954.
7. Hearings and reports of the U.S. House Committee on Un-American Activities, Senate Internal Security Subcommittee, and Senate Committee on Government Operations. Report of the Canadian Royal Commission, June 27, 1946.

Report of the Australian Royal Commission, August 22, 1955.

8. U.S. Senate Internal Security Subcommittee, *Interlocking Subversion in Government Departments*, 1953, p. 3.

9. Page, Leitch & Knightley, *The Philby Conspiracy*, 1968, p. 192.

10. U.S. House Committee on Un-American Activities, *Security Practices in the National Security Agency*, Aug. 13, 1962.

11. John Bulloch and Henry Miller, *Spy Ring: The Full Story of the Naval Secrets Case*, 1961. Arthur Tietjen, *Soviet Spy Ring*, 1961. E. H. Cookridge, *The Third Man*, 1968.

12. *Time*, Apr. 21 & Apr. 28, 1961.

13. *Life Magazine*, Apr. 26, 1968, p. 30.

14. U.S. Senate Internal Security Subcommittee, *The Wennerstroem Spy Case*, 1964.

15. "The Country That Saved Itself," *Reader's Digest*, Nov. 1964.

16. AP Dispatch, La Paz, July 26, 1968.

17. Colonel Oleg Penkovskiy, *The Penkovskiy Papers*, 1965, p. 102.

18. Ibid., p. 84.

19. Ibid., p. 268.

20. Ibid., p. 184.

21. Ibid., Chapter 3.

22. Commander Guy Richards, *Imperial Agent*, 1966, p. 20.

23. The Otepka Brief placed in the *Congressional Record*, Dec. 14, 1967. See also, *Congressional Record*, Oct. 19, 1967, p. S15033.

24. *The Worker*, Nov. 16, 1965.

25. 39 U.S. Code #4354.

26. *Sunshine Publishing Company v. Summerfield*, 184 F. Supp. 767, 772.

27. 1 L.Ed. 2nd 2208.

28. *Corinth Publications, Inc. v. Wesberry*, 388 U.S. 448. Senate Judiciary Committee, Hearings on Abe Fortas, July 11-23, 1968, p. 1267.

29. *Harry Schackman v. California*, 388 U.S. 454.

30. 258 F. Supp. 983.

31. *Saul Landau v. Chief of Police of Berkeley, California*, 388 U.S. 456, *Ginsberg v. New York*, 20 L.Ed. 195, and *Kenneth Jacobs v. New York*, 388 U.S. 431.

X. The Solution — Political Action

1. U.S. News & World Report, May 29, 1967, p. 21.

2. Dr. Anthony Kubek, *How The Far East Was Lost*, 1963.

3. See Schlafly & Ward, *The Gravediggers*, p. 73.

4. Exclusively revealed in Schlafly, *A Choice Not An Echo*.

About the Authors—

PHYLLIS SCHLAFLY is the author of the best-sellers *A Choice Not An Echo* and *Safe — Not Sorry*, and co-author with Admiral Ward of *The Gravediggers* and *Strike From Space*. Her study of military affairs dates from World War II when she was a ballistics gunner and technician at the largest ammunition plant in the world.

Mrs. Schlafly is the mother of six children, and is a Phi Beta Kappa with a Master's Degree in Political Science from Radcliffe College.

In naming her "Woman of Achievement in Public Affairs," the *St. Louis Globe-Democrat* said: "Phyllis Schlafly stands for everything that has made America great and for those things which will keep it that way."

REAR ADMIRAL CHESTER WARD, USN (Ret.), BS, LLB, LLM, was Judge Advocate General of the U.S. Navy, 1956-60. In 1968 he received the degree of Juris Doctor, with highest honors, from George Washington University Law School.

He has lectured on national strategy in seminars conducted by the U.S. Army, Stanford Research Institute, the Institute for American Strategy, and the University of Pennsylvania. He is a founding member of the National Strategy Committee, American Security Council.

Admiral Ward was awarded the Legion of Merit by President Eisenhower for his contributions to the effective use of United States seapower and his "realistic" opposition to "the Communist conspiracy."

PERE MARQUETTE PRESS
P. O. Box 495, Alton, Illinois 62002

Enclosed find $_____ for _____ copies of

THE BETRAYERS by Phyllis Schlafly & Chester Ward

1 copy	$1	(including postage)
3 copies	$2	100 copies $30
10 copies	$5	500 copies $125
25 copies	$10	1,000 copies $200

Illinois residents add 5% sales tax

Name_____
(please print)

Street_____

City_____

State_____ Zip_____

For your convenience, you may use this form to order other books by
Phyllis Schlafly and Admiral Ward at the same prices listed above:

How many copies?

Safe — Not Sorry   _____

Strike from Space   _____

A Choice Not An Echo   _____

The Gravediggers   _____

Amount enclosed $_____ Total copies _____

MAR 22 1972

The Issue

is

Survival

Give
THE BETRAYERS

To Friends and Neighbors, whether Republicans, Democrats or Independents. In politics there is no substitute for door-to-door precinct work.

Ask doctors to give this book to their patients, employers to their employees, parents to college and high school students. Give it to opinionmakers such as editors, radio and TV commentators, clergymen, teachers, writers, and elected officials. Give it to members of your church, club, union or fraternity. Distribute it at meetings, on trains, in motels. Ask your local newsstands, bookstores and libraries to carry it.

Use order form on reverse side.

POLITICS IS EVERYBODY'S BUSINESS!

Do your part in this educational effort while there is still time to . . .

KEEP THE PEACE

by

KEEPING AMERICA STRONG

PERE MARQUETTE PRESS

P. O. Box 495   Alton, Illinois 62002